THE ODD SQUAD'S

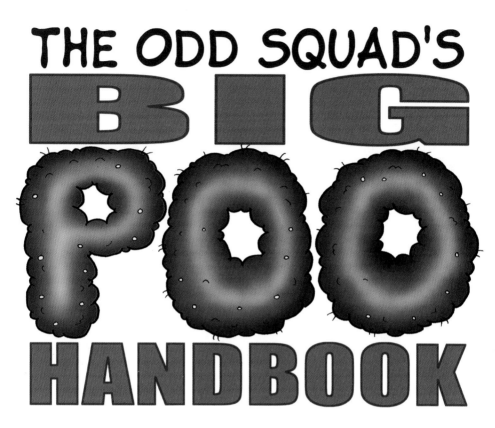

BIG POO HANDBOOK

by Allan and Becky Plenderleith

This book is dedicated to: sprouts, cabbage, baked beans, curry, lager, prunes, turkey, laxatives, lentils, bran, dysentery, OAP incontinence, fast food outlets, and red bills.

Acknowledgements:
hands, toilet tissue, wet wipes, washing machines, stain removers, bleach, bonfires, and second-hand shops.

RAVETTE PUBLISHING

JOIN OUR PETITION NOW!

This book, The Odd Squad's Big Poo Handbook is a
work of great, creative genius, regardless of its
working class subject matter, poo-poo.

Harass the middle class judges of The Booker Prize
to consider this epic tomb for the 2004 competition.

Complete the form below and send to
Colman Getty PR, Middlesex House, 34-42 Cleavand St. London.

I.................................of................................
hereby declare that The Odd Squad's Big Poo
Handbook is a work of such outstanding beauty
that it should be immediately considered for
The Booker Prize. Acknowledge its rightful
place in history now....or watch your doorstep!

First published in 2003 by
Ravette Publishing Limited
Unit 3, Tristar Centre
Star Road, Partridge Green
West Sussex RH13 8RA

THE ODD SQUAD and all related characters
© 2003 by Allan Plenderleith
www.theoddsquad.co.uk

Printed in Belgium by Proost

ISBN: 1 84161 168 9

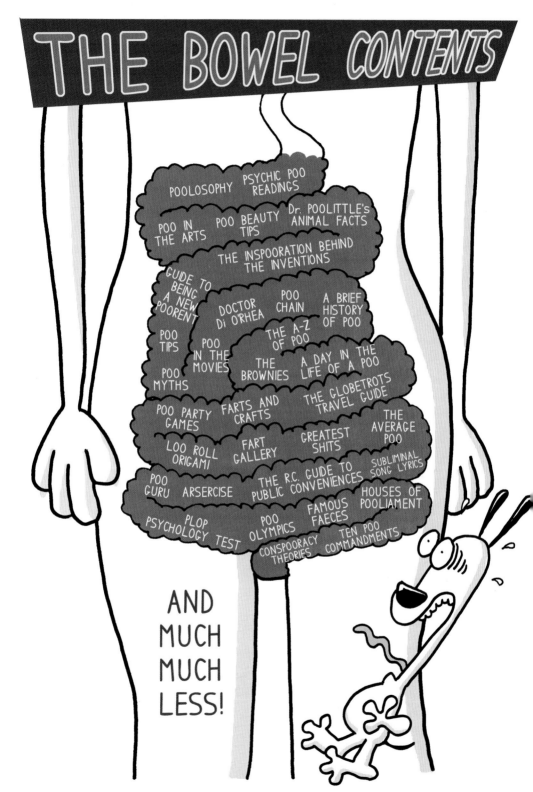

A BRIEF HISTORY OF POO!

Forget school/university/grandparent versions of history. hokum pokum. Lies, damned lies. 'They' don't want you to know The Truth. But we don't give a stuff. here's what <u>really</u> happened in the anals of history...

THE BIG BANG

Chemicals swirling around in one explosive cocktail? Pah! One day God was on the crapper after a night out on the clouds and, woosh, got the trots. Nine poops later and the solar system was formed, the sun being God's red-sore sphincter!

god's anus

uranus

The DINOSAUR AGE

Finally the truth about the extinction of dinosaurs! As they became bigger and bigger, so did their poos. Soon they were up to their necks in their own bum sludge. In the baking heat it soon hardened around them, trapping them there until they died. Stupid lizards.

The DAWN OF MAN

Millions of years later, when monkeys were throwing their own banana-scented faeces at themselves, one particular ape refused to touch his own poo, preferring to wipe his bum with a palm leaf and spray the air with magnolia pollen — and mankind was born!

The EGYPTIANS

Civilised society the Egyptians – they had a penchant for Toblerone. however, this resulted in triangular poos (no wonder they walked funny). Lacking a decent sewage system, the Egyptian wideboy Tootandcomin (so called because he would always fart before he asked people to 'come in') ordered his people to stack their poos somewhere in the desert. The resulting poop pile became the wonderful pyramids!

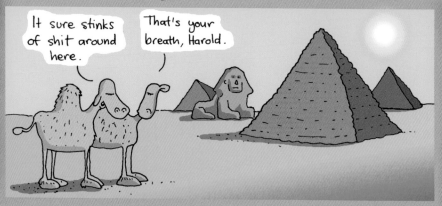

The VIKINGS

Often falsely accused of being 'hairy horny marauders' the Vikings were actually soft pansies with a fondness for synchronised rowing with a poor sense of direction getting lost often (blondes you see). They were too girly to 'log overboard' so they had to wait until they reached land then run screaming with bulging pants to the nearest settlement, scaring the crap out of the locals.

1066 The Battle of Poostings

Two silly armies of men were fighting about who took the last sheet of loo roll when King Harold got struck in the eye by a U.F.O. (Unusual Faecal Obelisk) and after a rather nasty eye infection, died of embarrassment.

The Brownish-Black Plague

The story goes that Marco Polo, from his travels in the Far East, brought back the world's first Chinese takeaway. By the time it reached our shores, however, the sweet and sour "chicken" with fried rice was heaving with disease, but divvy Marco foolishly warmed it up in the oven and ate it anyway. Soon Marco ran into the street screaming with Brownish Black diarrhoea spraying out of his behind. The deadly disease spread across Europe like a DJ Otzi record. Many died.

1666 The Great Poo of London

It started in Smeggy Lane, at a Baker's when the Youth Training Scheme lad forgot to wash his hands after squeezing his zits. Then he made a batch of YumYums which sold like hot doughnuts, triggering a snowball effect of upset tummies. People were pooping directly onto the pavements and into each others' pockets. But then, Mrs Cawley lit a match to deal with all that gas and toxic fumes. Boom! (NB: London still smells of poo to this day!)

1920's POOhIBITION

In America during the trotting twenties, people were pooing far too much, so the president of the time, Jimmy Carter, decided to ban pooping. But this merely encouraged mafia-like poop-legging where people would pay to go on illicit buckets under the moonshine.

1969 First Poo on the Moon

Neil Arsestrong was the first man to lay a cable on another planet.
Apparently Neil's poos looked remarkably similar to golden eagles, hence
the phrase: 'The Eagle has landed.' As Neil stepped onto the planet for
the first time, he released an enormous poop, uttering the immortal line:
'One small step for man, one giant poop for mankind.'

1980's Poo Mountains

As a consequence of famine in third world countries, there was a
shortage of poo in these undeveloped zones. Thankfully, the well-fed
developed world stepped in, shipping huge mountains of western
excrement to supplement their poop drought. Aren't we kind!

Poo in the Arts

Poo has been an inspiration to artists for centuries: from the early drawings of cavemen having a dump (hmm, wonder what they used for paint?) to every entry in the Turner Prize. So let's take a stroll through the anals of art history.

The Moaning Lisa

Many have pondered upon the reason behind 'The Moaning Lisa's' strange expression. Has she managed to lay a 3 foot cable without it breaking off? Has the splash from a malteser poo just gone up her bum? Or has she got piles? We will never know. Displayed in the Loo Gallery in Paris.

Moaning Lisa

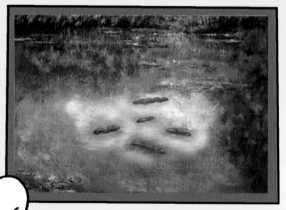

Poos in Clouds

An early work by Money, a part-time toilet attendant. He found there wasn't a big demand for paintings of the filthy poo-ridden rivers of France, so went on to paint pretty pictures of lily-pads instead.

(though if the paint is stripped off you will find poops sneakily painted underneath)

Millionaire artist Damien 'Omen' Hearse created huge controversy (and piles of cash) with this piece. Some say it's about 'society's duality when confronted with the truth of existence'. Others think it's just crap.

Andy Sorehole's Poo Copies

Wacky white-haired Sorehole thought that photocopying pictures of poo and colouring them in with crayon was really clever, suggesting that although we all think we are unique individuals, our poos are all identical and therefore we are all part of a greater 'oneness'. But that's rubbish! We all know every poo is completely different like those sweetcorn ones, or the ones with jaggy bits or the ones that you need to wipe forever...

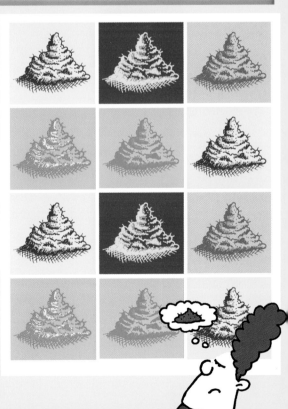

Poo in Unmade Bed

Vodka-breath 'artist' Tracey Eminem came up with this effort after a big night on the Liefraumilch.   She awoke to find the heap still steaming on the sheets but claims it wasn't hers (yeah, right). Some fool bought it for a million which she spent immediately on a Smirnoff factory.

Poocasso's Log

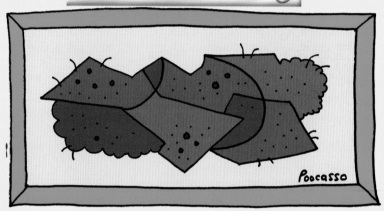

Poocasso

Sitting on the loo wondering what he could cut off to make himself famous in the art world, Poocasso dropped this baby down the pan. Once he (and his sphincter) had recovered from the shock, the poo's bizarre shape inspired him to create a new art form - cubism! All that from simply eating too many crisps!

Dali's Melted Poos

Salivate Dali, the Spanish painter, was extremely fond of garlic. The problem was his breath was absolutely rank (even curling his moustache) and consequently everything he tried to paint actually melted, hence the famous 'melted poos'. His career ended when one day he accidentally ate a tic tac.

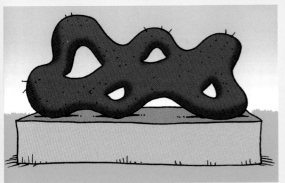

Henry Poore

Henry Poore, the English sculptor, was addicted to curly wurlies. So much so that his poos began to resemble the twisted chocolate treat. He produced large sculptures of these master poos. Academics thought they looked like women and stuff, and bingo - he made the big time!

Jackson Bollock

The world's worst artist, Jackson Bollock, was so bad at art he actually pooed on his own artwork in frustration. Unfortunately, one poncey art critic saw the result, hailed it a masterpiece by a troubled mind (troubled sphincter more like!), and subsequently Jackson was deemed a genius. He wasn't. He was just an ordinary guy with a sore arse.

JACKSON BOLLOCK

HMM, I SEE EIGHT PINTS OF LAGER, CHEAP ALCOPOPS AND A DODGY KEBAB.

Poolosophers

What's the meaning of life? Why are we here?
What's love got to do, got to do with it? It's all about Poo! Dur.

PLATO

One of Dizney's most loveable characters, Plato is the founder of all poolosophy. He realised that all objects in the physical world merely resemble poos. For example, a chair is really a stool; a tree is really a log etc.

A LOG   A STOOL   A TURTLEHEAD

ARCHIMEDES

The greatest poolosopher of all time. Whilst in the bath trying to make bubbles, Archimedes let one slip out. So, Archimedes discovered that if you poo in the bath, the same amount of water is displaced. Genius.

Eureka!

KANT

Kant invented pooniversal theory: the notion that you cannot be sure of other people's pooing experience, only your own. Not so. You can quite easily spy on other people on the toilet by drilling a hole in toilet cubicle walls!

Hello!

NIETZSCHE

Nietzsche hypoothesized that the basic human drive is the will to poo and that societal doctrines like religious hygiene and moral decorum suppress this base instinct. Nietzsche also theorized that life is meaningless without poo and only the superhuman pooer who lives to shit has meaning.

I have the power!

MARX

Marx guessed that the economic cisterns of a period affects the faecal organisations of the time. In looman's terms, if you sit on an expensive loo like at Harruds, your working class bum will be too embarrassed to dump its load.

I'm not worthy

FREUD

Freud invented psychopooanalysis: the interpretation of our dreams....they're all about poo. eg: if you dream of falling you will experience brown Niagra in the morning.

I dreamt I pooed the bed.

Houses of Pooliament

LAWS TO BE PASSED:

The use of air fresheners to be made illegal as there is nothing more confusing and disappointing than inhaling the strangely magnolia fragranced stench of poop (let's face it, all fresheners whatever their 'perfume' smell of old lady magnolia). At least you know where you are with your own, natural eau de crap.

SNIFF!

SNIFF!

?

18 degrees.... perfect!

Leaving a skid mark on the toilet bowl to be made compulsory so that it can serve as a warning system for the next visitor. The skid indicates how warm the seat is, as over time flushing erodes your faecal signature, thereby revealing the temperature of the seat, and whether to sit (if warm) or hover (if chilly).

Eugh!

Leaving a turd bobbing to be made a hangable offence. Literally. The offending turd will be used for DNA identification and then hung around the culprit's shameless neck like a leper bell. proving to the constipated masses that this person is a braggart and a show off.

Leaving the toilet seat up (if male/lesbian) or down (if female/gayboy) to be prohibited as the precious time spent arguing over this is hugely wasteful and could be spent comparing notes regarding performance. Consequently, seats shall be abolished. Women prefer to hover anyway – it's thigh toning!

MUSEUM

WOW!

WHITEUS CRUSTIUS

The collection of dog craps by overly-hygienic owners in poop-a-scoopers to be banned as a whole generation of youngsters are being deprived the chance to marvel at white pavement blobs.

I'd like to pass a motion!

ORDER! ORDER!

Beef vindaloo and a plain naan.

SNORE!

The Inspooration BEHIND
the Inventions!

For centuries, mankind has attributed the world's greatest inventions to the selfless desire by the brilliant few to improve the quality of life for the masses. Pff! It's all about crapping...

FIRE (21 July something BC)

Caveman Uga Booga invented fire as he idly rubbed two twigs together waiting for a bout of constipation to pass (all those herbivorian banquets) and realised it was also an hilarious way to maximise fart entertainment!

THE TELEPHONE (1876)

Sir Alexander Graham Bell invented the telephone so that we can ring our friends and brag about the size of our poops. Nowadays we use the phone to call our friends when we know that they'll be mid-strain on the loo, eg: 8am and 2.47pm. Ha!

The LIGHTBULB (1879)

Thomas Edison invented the lightbulb to encourage people not to poop in the wrong place in the dark of the night. Killjoy.

The AIRPLANE (1903)

Orville (yes, the duck - he's always been interested in flying, right up to the sky) and Wilbur Wright invented the first passenger aircraft to enable them to fly over conurbations and drop poo bombs on unsuspecting passers-by. And you thought that was bird crap on your car.

The TELEVISION (1926)

Saint John Logie Baird invented the television to help us pass the time between craps. Join the crusade to have him canonized now.

The LAVATORY (1876)

Thomas Crapper invented the toilet as a private health spa for poos with plunge pool, pine aromatherapy treatments and Jacuzzi.

CHain

incontinent granny

vegetarian

Discharges 4.5 km^2 field of manure daily. (Resulting gas clouds are actual cause of hole in ozone.)

blue whale

15 tonne poop, once per annum. Whale is in fact blue due to extreme straining.

evil cat

Volume of poop is irrelevant as just 1 millilitre emits a toxic, lethal stench.

HSSSSSSS

slug

That's no slug trail - but one long skidmark. Respect.

baby

Rank lowered because babies get someone else to wipe their bum (unfair advantage).

horsey

Difficult to ascertain as only craps when walking on roads. Poo gets lost in car tyre treads.

politician

63.07 m^2 of verbal diarrhoea per sentence.

BLAH BLAH BLAH BLAH BLAH

THE AVERAGE POO!

Of course, there's no such thing as an average poo, they're all special. Like snowflakes, no two poos are the same. But here's some "fascinating" statistics anyway.

THE AVERAGE POO WEIGHS 6.8 GRAMS

THE AVERAGE POO IS PANTONE COLOUR REFERENCE 319-4

THE AVERAGE POO IS HOME TO 1,974 933 BACTERIA AWH... BLESS.

THE AVERAGE POO SPENDS 204 HOURS IDLING THE TIME AWAY BEFORE LAUNCH IN THE BOWEL

THE AVERAGE POO IS 6.5CM LONG AND 4.84CM IN GIRTH ...LONGER THAN THE AVERAGE PENIS

THE AVERAGE POO CONSISTS OF 56% CARBOHYDRATE, 22% PROTEIN, 0.02% SATURATED FAT, 0.00004 UNSATURATED FAT, 37% SWEETCORN

THE AVERAGE POO WANTS TO BE AN ASTRONAUT WHEN IT GROWS UP

THE AVERAGE POO HAS 3.4 REGRETS

THE AVERAGE POO REQUIRES 3.7 WIPES

THE AVERAGE POO OF A VEGETARIAN REQUIRES 15.3 WIPES

THE AVERAGE POO CREATES ENOUGH SPLASHBACK TO SOAK 5 SHEETS OF 2-PLY LOO ROLL

THE AVERAGE POO DISPLAYS 134 FISSURES - MORE THAN THE SURFACE OF 1/873TH OF THE MOON

THE AVERAGE POO TAKES 2.7 DAYS TO REACH THE SEWAGE PLANT

THE AVERAGE POO LEAVES 27MM OF SKID ON THE TOILET BOWL

THE AVERAGE POO SMELLS LIKE 'HI KARATE' AFTERSHAVE 6 YEARS PAST ITS 'USE BY' DATE

THE AVERAGE POO HAS BEEN WITH 12 FARTS

Doctor Poolittle's
AMAZING ANIMAL FACTS!

THE AVERAGE ELEPHANT CRAPS 57,828 TONNES IN ITS LIFETIME. IN CAPTIVITY, THIS RISES TO 148,937 TONNES (AND 4 OZ) DUE TO EXCESSIVE PEANUT INTAKE.

GOLDFISH HAVE PSYCHOLOGICAL DETACHMENT ISSUES REGARDING SEPARATION FROM THEIR MOTHERS, WHICH IS WHY THEY NEVER FULLY RELEASE A POO FROM THEIR BUMS.

A PIGEON ONLY HITS ONE WINDSCREEN IN ITS LIFETIME.

SPLAT!

HAMSTERS ONLY POO WHEN THEIR CAGES HAVE JUST BEEN CLEANED.

SNAKES DO NOT, IN FACT, EXIST. THEY ARE ACTUALLY THE ZOMBIE POOPS OF THE BLACK PANTHER. YOU SEE, THE PANTHER IS ALWAYS IN A HURRY AND EATS FAR TOO QUICKLY. THE UNDIGESTED FOOD MATTER IS HALF ALIVE WHEN IT IS EXCRETED! COOL. JEALOUS?

AS DOGS GET OLDER, THEIR POO TURNS WHITE - HENCE WHITE COILS ON THE PAVEMENT. YOUNG DOGS HAVE THE ENERGY TO CONCEAL THEIR TURDS IN THE HEDGES!

DID YOU KNOW?... CHIPMUNKS DON'T HAVE COLONS. WHICH IS WHY THEY STORE THEIR POO IN THEIR CHEEKS!

≥ SQUELCH ≤ HA HA HA!

≥ SPLAT ≤ HAHA HA!

≥ SPURT ≤ HAHAHA!

WHY DO HYENAS LAUGH? THEY ACTUALLY "SUFFER" FROM UNRELENTING BUT HILARIOUS WET FARTS ALL DAY LONG!

IF ONE LEMMING GOES TO THE TOILET, ALL THE OTHER LEMMINGS FOLLOW SUIT. IN 1943, A COPYCAT OF LEMMINGS CAUSED AN AVALANCHE IN THE SWISS TOWN OF ST. LAURENT. MANY DIED.

THE PEACOCK RAISES ITS ELABORATE TAIL - NOT TO WOO PROSPECTIVE HENS - BUT TO DETRACT ATTENTION FROM THE FACT IT HAS THE TROTS... THE DOWNSIDE OF A SEED-RICH DIET.

PLOP!

SQUIRT!

Ooh, isn't he lovely!

THE LOCH NESS MONSTER IS A CASE OF MISTAKEN IDENTITY - IT IS ACTUALLY THE HUGE TURD OF THE CONSTIPATED NATIVE HIGHLAND COW!

THE INFAMOUS BLACK WIDOW SPIDER ACTUALLY KILLS HER 'PARTNER' FOR FORGETTING TO PUT THE LEAF SEAT DOWN.

I promise I won't do it again!

Ketchup?

FLEAS FIND IT IMPOSSIBLE TO POOP IN THE PRESENCE OF OTHER FLEAS, AND THAT'S WHY THEY FEEL ITCHY - THEY'RE JIGGING ABOUT ON THE SPOT!

THE CHAMELEON ONLY EVOLVED TO BLEND INTO ITS SURROUNDINGS TO EVADE SCOLDINGS DUE TO ITS PENCHANT FOR COMPULSIVE CRAPPING IN OTHER CREATURES' HOUSES...

BAD BOY!

Poo Myths

Myth: if you don't wash your hands after you've been to the toilet you will get stomach ache

FACT

incorrect. you <u>will</u> get a fashionable brown shade of nail varnish!

Do you like my nails

WIFF!

Ooh! They're.... .... oh AKH!

Myth: if you watch your partner going for a dump, they will lose their romantic allure.

FACT

chances are, they've already lost it (especially if you've been together for more than 2 weeks)

Hi!

 **Myth:** if you have diarrhoea you must replace lost fluids with plenty of water.

 **Fact**

Nah. don't bother. It's the only time you'll experience that mr. universe muscle definition!

If he doesn't drink soon he'll die.

Yeah, but look at those abs!

Myth: if you try to look between your legs to watch yourself dumping and the wind changes, you'll stay that way.

Fact

It's true actually! try it!

She must be in the circus.

 **Myth:** if you strain too hard, you will get piles.

Fact

false. but your innards may be forced out.

Phone the doctor.

THE TEN POO COMMANDMENTS

1. Thou shalt not kill off a turd mid-delivery!

2. Thou shalt not steal the last sheet of toilet roll without replacing it - unless, of course, you are in a friend's house!

3. Thou shalt not covet another man's turds!

4. Thou shalt not commit adultery with another man's toilet!

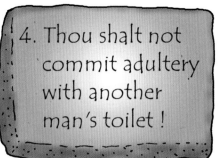

5. Thou shalt not take the Turd's name in vain!

6. Thou shalt not poo on a Sunday!

7. Thou shalt not disrespect thy mother and father's incontinence!

8. Thou shalt not give false evidence to thy neighbour!

9. Thou shalt not have any other turds than me!

10. Thou shalt not construct effigies in my image!

THE 7 DEADLY POO SINS

1.
NEVER CROSS A PARK IN HIGH HEELS!

2.
NEVER ROLL DOWN A HILL WITH CAREFREE ABANDON!

3.
NEVER BEND BACK TOO FAR TO SMELL YOUR OWN FARTS!

4.
BEFORE BLOWING OFF IN SHORTS, ALWAYS MAKE SURE IT'S NOT A WET ONE!

5.
NEVER HOLD YOUR POOS IN FOR TOO LONG!

6.
NEVER FOLLOW THROUGH IN THE SWIMMING BATHS!

7.
NEVER BLOW OFF WHILST IN THE DOGGY POSITION

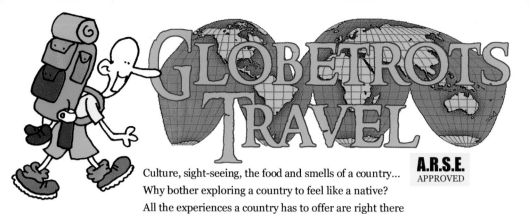

GLOBETROTS TRAVEL

Culture, sight-seeing, the food and smells of a country...
Why bother exploring a country to feel like a native?
All the experiences a country has to offer are right there
on their crappers ...

FRANCE

RESORT DESCRIPTION:

The Eyeful Tower is indeed an impressive
structure - it has taken years to create. Be
prepared to wait in a queue for ages, and
once it's your turn to go, the experience
will cost you dearly - in pride.

SNIFF

What a
marvellous
bouquet!

A
FRENCH
TOILET

FACILITIES:

None outside of Paris. Real French
people are content to poop into holes in the
ground they call "toilettes" which translated,
means "English go home". No wonder they
invented the bidet - it completes the unhygienic
humiliating ritual.

ACTIVITIES/SPORTS:

Avoid your own water sports (see above).
Take plastic bags to protect your shoes.

EXCURSIONS:

Nip across the channel to Kent where
they have proper toilets.

MEALS:

Never eat anything made by a local - anyone who
doesn't mind pooping in a hole clearly can't wash their
hands prior to food preparation. Nouveau cuisine began
in France because tiny portions of food minimises the
frequency of defecation.

A FRENCH "BAGUETTE"

(STRONG GARLIC SMELL)

SPAIN

A TYPICAL SPANISH RESORT

99% ENGLISH TOURISTS

85% POO

89% Germans

RESORT DESCRIPTION:

Just like home, but with sunburn. You can find more English food in coastal Spain than you can in England. Tourism has been specifically developed by the Spanish Tourist Bored on the Coast to allow inebriated British people to poo directly into the sea (or drown).

MEALS:

Local tapas is a bit like oily finger food and is ideal for sharing (sharing!!?) ... a dysentery whammy. Eat only congealing English grub so at least you'll be familiar with your holiday belly symptoms.

FACILITIES:

It won't matter because you'll be too pissed or sick with sunstroke to even notice!

ENTERTAINMENT:

Revel in the individual performances of fellow guests heaving and squeezing all hours. Life is a cabaret my chum.

EXCURSIONS:

Bars - for rehydration purposes only of course - besides, toilets are always conveniently located nearby.

WAFT

AKH!

PONG!

AFRICA

RESORT DESCRIPTION:
Wide open boring spaces with some shrubbery to help conceal bouts of diarrhoea (or the dead bodies of people who commit tv-withdrawal hari kari). Accommodation often features mud huts... you don't wanna know where the 'mud' came from!

MEALS:
You may be tempted to indulge in huge chunks of locally farmed meat (très Waitrose) but freshness cannot be guaranteed. Instead, try joining a pack of lions for super-fresh meat!

ACTIVITIES:
SAFARI! In other words, a pretentious activity for Guardian-reading liberals with a perversion for watching big game animals pooing. Don't get too close to the elephants - remember the splatter zone!

EXCURSIONS:
Hospital.

ENTERTAINMENT:
If the squits are surprisingly late in coming, amuse yourself with swatting huge malaria-riddled mosquitoes. They will win.

INDIA

WHICH IS A PLATE OF CURRY AND WHICH IS A PLATE OF POO?

ANSWER: CURRY AND POO ARE THE SAME THING!

RESORT DESCRIPTION:
A Mecca for Poo worshippers - 98% of visitors will enjoy a bout of Delhi Belly (the remaining 2% are victims of spontaneous combustion).

SPORTS:
Sprinting - to the "toilet", the sink, anywhere other than the sanctity of your cleanish bed.

WOULD YOU LIKE THE SQUELCHY SQUIRTS, THE RING OF FIRE, THE EXTREME FLATULENCE OR THE EXPLODING ARSE?

CAN WE HAVE A BIT OF EACH?

FACILITIES:
You'll be able to provide your own air conditioning system with extreme flatulence - you can make a small fortune hiring yourself out to fellow tourists. You'll also be able to provide your own pool... of sweat, excretions and tears - again, hire yourself out to appreciative tourists!

MEALS:
Eat? Eat? You won't even be able to hold down "bottled" water.

EXCURSIONS:
Air ambulance home.

EXCHANGE RATES

1 drop of local water	1 pint of diarrhoea
1 salad washed with goat pee	4 days in a local hospital
1 street vendor snack	1 sphincter transplant
1 swig of locally made beer	1 flight home in coffin
1 snog with local	1 brush with death

POOCIPITATION CHART
Average Poo Fall

INDIA · AFRICA · FRANCE · SPAIN · USA · UK

HOLIDAY HEALTH TIPS (for maximum poo action):
· Remember to add plenty of ice to drinks
· Wait until the end of meal times and gorge on the stagnant, crusting buffet
· Don't forget to forget to wash hands after going to toilet
· Use only tap water (or toilet water if you're clever) to brush teeth
· Don't spit out any water swallowed in swimming pool - think of it as a free non-alcoholic cocktail
· Don't take up valuable potential duty-free space in luggage with diarrhoea pills - a visit to the local hospital is like a mini holiday within a holiday. And you get room service!

EMERGENCY Language Guide!

Forget "Please" and "Thank you" and "Where is the library", there's only phrase you need to know when travelling abroad:

"I HAVE A TURTLEHEAD - WHERE IS THE SHITTER?"

Scottish:	Eey ha uh toot'lheed - whe ees de shi'er?
Irish:	Gisanot'erGuinness
Yobbish:	I have a turtlehead - wanna see it?
Welsh:	Ca a turtlehead - ble ydy 'r shitter?
French:	Zut alors! J'ai un turtlehead - où est le shitter?
Spanish:	Tengo un turtlehead - dónde el shitter es?
Italian:	Mama mia, ho un turtlehead - dove lo shitter é?
Jamaican:	Hey… man… I have a turtlehead
Norwegian:	phlegm, jeg har ent - er hvor shitter?
German:	Ich habe ein shizha - wo ist der shitter?
Greek:	Ew va en poopoo - no evai o shitter?
Turkish:	I -si olmak a crappa nereye bkz be belguli tranimlik hela?
Slovenian:	Imam a turtlehead - kraj je drek?
Polish:	Mam pewien trtlhd - gdzie jest bagno?
Posh:	Book me a colonic on Harley Street, would you James
Baby:	Ga ga googoo ga gaaaa shitter?
Filipino:	ako may a turtlehead - saan ay ang shitter?
Latin:	Ego et a turlehead - qua est palus?
TXT:	':-(oooooooooo
Arabic:	????????????
Pissed:	Wahaturlwhuisthughshiii… (SFX: Splatter)
Amsterdamian:	tee hee tee hee hee hee hee hee hee tee hee tee hee tee hee teezzzzzzzzzzzzzzzzzzzzzzzzzzzz

 (cut out and keep)

R.C. TRAVEL GUIDE TO UK PUBLIC CONVENIENCES

Coloombus, Ridley Scott of the Antarsetic, Sore Walter Raleigh...travellers and explorers who braved uncharted lands in search of clean places to poop. They've all gone. So here's a dodgy guide to local WCs to do the dirty (few backhanders were accepted in the making of this guide).

McBURGER CHAINS

FACILITIES

The bare minimum. Several cubicles featuring single WC suites - though a number will be either blocked, impressively filthy, or the door engagingly broken or occupied by old ladies who can't lock the door. En suite basins will feature scalding water and sticky soap that never washes off. Hand dryers, if electric, feature a micro laboratory of deadly germ warfare; or the towel roll will already be strangely soaking; or individual paper towel dispenser will tantalisingly feature a small triangle of paper that you just can't pull. Single sex rooms only and women's options will feature sanitary bins that are overflowing. Men's option will be flooded... but not with water.

LOCATION

...its only plus. These bog standard facilities are everywhere - with the added bonus that you can eat whilst you defecate.

Turd rating:

PUBLIC TOILETS

FACILITIES

Usually Victorian in design, prehistoric in sanitation, "Gentlemen's" urinals will feature the discolouration of an alcoholic, toffee-eating smoker and curious holes drilled in the side panels of cubicles. Whilst the "Ladies" will feature scary, elevated cubicle side doors from where ghostly hands appear begging for paper (that's if you've made it through the pain barrier of old granny piss stench). ∗

LOCATION

The usual hunting ground for the above - car parks and lonely scenic spots in local parks. Only recommended for use if you are an adrenalin junkie.

∗Public Conveniences are very popular choices with gay men and murderers. Special offers may be available.

Turd rating: MINUS

SHOPPING CENTRE

FACILITIES

The usual... broken cubicles, splashed toilet seats, mis-spelt graffiti but with the additional service of piped music to cover the splattering sound effects of fellow customers. You may also enjoy the added excitement of thick people trying to open your door despite the lock clearly displaying an "Engaged" notice. Also features an idle attendant who appears to be physically unable to flush offending floaters ('offending' only because they're not your own). Revel in the huge smudge-ridden mirrors featuring teenage girls daubing their eyes in kohl, and teenage boys squeezing their zits.

LOCATION

Always the furthest possible distance when you realise you're wetting yourself, regardless of where you are. **Turd rating:**

PUBLIC HOUSES

FACILITIES

Like home from home - very comfy surrounds with carpet, curtains and the over-use of air fresheners to mask the permanent aroma of beer, puke and fags. Customers may also enjoy the added luxury of a condom machine (though you will have to provide your own partner). Or an American-tan tight machine (though you may not have the old lady legs to properly display them).

LOCATION

In towns and cities, approx every 30 drunken stumbles, but you may feel the need to purchase an alcoholic beverage (or ten) to alleviate your guilt over abusing their facilities for "patrons only" (oh well). Alternatively, run like the wind past landlord. In villages and hamlets, you may experience "the locals" syndrome. Nettle-ridden roadside verges suddenly seem a welcoming option.

Turd rating:

HARRUDS

FACILITIES

Yeah, yeah, very nice gold plating but is any poop worth £1 a shot??!! Erm, well yes! Poops deserve the best!

LOCATION

No idea. Ask a tourist.

Turd rating:

DISABLED TOILETS

FACILITIES

Ahhhh, the crème de la crème of crappers. Spacious, clean facilities that have only ever been used 3 times before. Low level hand bars are excellent for gripping on to during constipation. And an emergency button should you require room service.

LOCATION

Surprisingly available all over the place.

Turd rating:

TOILETS AT OUTDOOR MUSIC FESTIVALS

FACILITIES

Everything the professional crapper needs: day-long queues to help build-up pleasure for eventual ejection; opportunity to spot/admire rival turtleheads; develop resourcefulness when it comes to wiping derrière with... apparently, nothing; the sheer thrill of not being able to 'go' when it's finally your turn; hand washer in the form of a pikey's dog... The list is endless - just like the endless diarrhoea you get free from the dodgy hippie burger stall.

LOCATION

Just follow the holy pilgrimage of sewage.

Turd rating:

poo beauty tips
with Maude Herzegova

A shamed to be seen in public with your plain poopie? Embarrassed by your poo's ordinary appearance? Jealous of your friends' glamorous by-products? Fret not. You too can be the proud owner of a showbiz shit. Just check into our excloosive health and pooty spa, The Sewery. Who knows, you may even end up insuring your booty-full poo for a million dollars...

PASTY POOS?

THE SOLOORIUM

It's so easy to enjoy the chocolate brown hue beloved by the rich and famous-ish? Just slip your poo on the Soloorium...

LAST SERVICE: JUNE 1974

TIPS:
- For the darkest, longest-lasting results book a fatal course of 10,000 100-minute sessions
- Occasionally remember to put goggles on your turd to prevent blindness in your turd's later life (and to create hilarious albino marks)
- Apply a tan accelerant for maximum streaking
- Always lock and barricade the door just in case a murderer tries to enter
- "Forget" that the Soloorium will make your turd age prematurely by decades
- If your poo turns Dreamguy orange, laugh at it *behind* its back

Pssssssss

BOGOIL

THE ST. TROPOO

Oops! I did it again!

TIPS:
- You MUST exfoliate your turd first with a bog brush before applying moisturiser
- Alternatively, dump your turd in a bath of creosote
- Now, as your turd looks like a minor celebrity, be prepared to go to the opening of a toilet bowl lid

You too can have poo as beautiful as pop princess Shitney Spears!

POO ACNE?

Are your poops plagued by sweetcorn acne? Embarrassed by seed and grain pimples? Don't suffer in silage! Simply apply endless amounts of Cream Mash to your digestive system and your poops will be as smooth as a baby's nappy (though sadly not as green).

BEFORE   AFTER

KISS

HAIRY POOPIES?

Inexplicable hair protusions? Furry faeces? Is it getting worse as you grow older? Dilapidation is the answer - just use whatever method gives you the most pain:

SHAVING
Just be careful not to flay your poop.

WAXING
Removing strips can be messy. Wear goggles.
WAX

PLUCKING
Use fingers, tweezers or teeth.

ELECTROLYSIS
Also creates a pleasant home-baking aroma.

SHAPELESS SHITS?

Are you mortified by your poop's flat, shapeless physique? Afraid it's not attractive to the opposite sect, pee? Join the tens of tens of poops who've had voluptuous Poop Jobs - a painful, scarring operation involving the insertion of leakable saline implants!

I'm in pain but I'm beautiful!

WRINKLY WOOPSIES?

If your poop is troubled with laughter lines and looks days older than its actual age, then try POOTOX... A simple lethal, oops that's *legal* injection that will smooth any wrinklage whilst preventing your faeces from making any expression whatsoever.

Using Pootox, you too can look like a tv presenter!

Poo Hair Dos

Poo has a far-retching influence in all aspects of everyday life. Even hair fashions - as seen recently on the catwalks of Pooris, Poo York and Poolan… It won't be long before everyone's asking for Jennifer Aniston's Rectal!

The Rectal

Long, flat, super-glossy turds that have been tamed with straightening irons and enhanced by a carb-free diet. Basically, the runs.

The Pellet

As modelled by celebrities such as Craig David and, er, Hamble.

The Princess Lay-a-Poo

Feel the force as you squeeze out these two perfect Cumberlands, attach to head with strawberry jam.

The Gareth Gates

Follow the 2-1-2 formation, cement with something wet and shiny, and the screaming will soon follow.

The Rapunzel

A look mostly worn by old ladies who are unaware that they're going to the poo, and also, too infirm to break off and wipe the detritus.

The Mohican Skid

A touching look worn by guys who lift their girlfriends on to their shoulders at music concerts.

The Beckham

Long or short, it doesn't matter, so long as your mousy barnet is crowned with yellow streaks (just eat plenty of custard).

The Constipator

When everything's backed up down there, go sans hair for that Eastend hardnut/Gayboy look!

Mystic Maude's

PSYCHIC POO Readings!

EVERY TURD TELLS A STORY, THEY ARE THE WINDOW OF THE SOUL... MYSTIC MAUDE CAN SEE YOUR FUTURE IN THE POO REMAINS LEFT BEHIND IN THE BOWL...

ALWAYS THE BRIDESMAID, NEVER THE BRIDE WHO SQUANDERED MORE THAN £9K ON A PRETTY AVERAGE WEDDING. TIGHT FISTED, AS WELL AS TIGHT ARSED, YOU'LL FIND CAREER NIRVANA AS AN ACCOUNTANT. IN LOVE, YOU'RE DESTINED TO DIE ALONE.

A FLOATER THROUGH LIFE, YOU JUST LIKE TO BOB ALONG. YOU'RE PRONE TO OUTSTAY YOUR WELCOME - SOME ATTRIBUTE THIS TO A MEAN STREAK, BUT IT'S ACTUALLY DUE TO A FEAR OF SOLITUDE. IDEALLY, YOU SHOULD SEEK WORK IN A SEA-LIFE CENTRE AS AN EXHIBIT - YOU THRIVE ON THE ADULATION OF AN AUDIENCE AND YOU LOVE TO RETURN FOR AN ENCORE.

An introverted exhibitionist by nature, you hate to be seen in public without a shroud. You're so showbiz, even your offspring (those little poops that are born once you thought you'd finished) must be veiled. You're unhappy with your appearance (too brown) and will resort to plarsetic surgery. But at least you're pals with the Sultana of Brown Eye.

You can't help but be a drama queen. You always have to go one better than everyone else. Brag brag brag is all you do. But it's obvious you've had a poop job - your ripples point in the wrong direction. So you're destined to find "success" as a corn star, and marry a taxidermist to help preserve your looks.

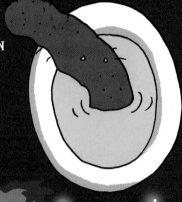

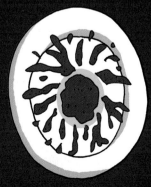

Yikes. You're a serial thriller - sneaking up on your unsuspecting victims without so much as a cramp as warning. Remorseless and without conscience, you can strike any time, any place, anywhere - leaving a trail of destruction and soreness. You'll probably turn into a drug addict (A-class laxatives) now you've got a taste for the splatter. And will never be monogamous, preferring to move casually from arse to arse. Some would call you a God.

Poo Tips
for the busy housewife!

PROBLEM:
Plagued by the vanishing turd? Feel cheated by its callous disappearing act?

Where's it gone?

SOLUTION:
Pad the plunge pool with ecologically-unfriendly amounts of loo roll to cushion its fall and present itself to you like a play-bunny on silken sheets.

FLASH!

Ooh! That's one to show the gran kids!

AAAH! COLD!

PROBLEM:
Is your husband constantly leaving the lavatory seat up, causing you untold emotional distress as your derrière meets cold wet ceramic?

SOLUTION:
Divorce.

PROBLEM:
Is your wife constantly leaving the lavatory seat up, causing you serious back strain with the constant lifting of disturbingly clean seats?

AAAR!

CRACK!

SOLUTION:
Cheat on her with a blonde bimbo.

YOU don't mind if I leave the toilet seat up, do you?

What's a toilet?

PUBLIC TOILET

PROBLEM:
Do you experience an irrational desire to use public conveniences whenever you see one, despite hating them?

SOLUTION:
Pants can withstand a moist turtlehead longer than you may imagine. Instead, visit an expensive restaurant for a superfluous meal and use their more uplifting facilities.

Table for two please.

BOKE!

PROBLEM:
Does someone keep leaving pubes on the toilet seat?

MUM! I WANT ONE!!

MIRKINS ALL SIZES!

SOLUTION:
Lucky you. Fashion the hairs into a mirkin and sell on the black market!

TOP 5 THINGS
that have happened to everyone in the **TOILET!**

1. The Disappearing Poo!

IT'S ALWAYS A BIG ONE BUT WHEN YOU LOOK ROUND IT'S GONE! NO-ONE CAN EXPLAIN THIS FRUSTRATING MYSTERY.

Where is it ?! I'm SURE I did one!

2. Splashback!

OCCURS WITH SMALL POOS. THEY CREATE A HUGE SPLASH COVERING YOU IN TOILET WATER. MOST UNPLEASANT.

AAA!

3. The Unflushable Poo!

DOES NOT BUDGE AFTER
REPEATED FLUSHING.
OPTIONS:

1. CHOP IT WITH A KNIFE.
2. FISH IT OUT WITH TONGS.
3. LIVE WITH IT.

4. The Reluctant Poo!

THE POO THAT COMES
OUT HALF WAY AND
STOPS. ONLY OPTION
IS TO SLICE IN HALF
WITH SPHINCTER.

5. The Neverending Wipe!

YOU KEEP ON WIPING BUT
YOU NEVER GET CLEAN!
YOU MAY BE THERE FOR
DAYS. (WORLD RECORD
STANDS AT 7 YEARS)

DOCTOR DI O'RHEA
for all your toilet troubles!

PATIENT: I can't stop imagining the Queen on the toilet. What's wrong with me?

Dr. O'Rhea: Nothing. Me too.

PATIENT: My wife says it's worth the extra 30p for premium toilet roll, is she right? Wouldn't cheaper, recycled paper be better for the planet?

Get a grip. Over the course of your lifetime, you're wasting £3984 on posh paper - that's the same as a 40inch plasma telly!

Every time I go for a whoopsie all I produce are perfectly formed rabbit droppings. It's so boring! What's up Doc?

Dr. O'Rhea: Hoppit!

PATIENT: You're my last resort. My boyfriend's driving me nuts with his inability to leave the toilet seat UP. What's wrong with him?

Dr. O'Rhea:

Durr, he's gay.

Patient:
I have a phobia about dropping my load in my friend's house in case I leave a smear. Any suggestions?

Dr. O'Rhea:
Why not start a profitable business as a pebble dash exterior specialist

Patient: Please help me. What can I do about my two-foot turds that just won't flush away?

Dr. O'Rhea:
Lucky git. Peddle your talents as a mini tourist attraction—advertise that the Loch Ness Monster has had babies!

Patient: My wife is obsessed with the bidet – she spends hours cleaning herself 'down there'. Is she a cleaning compulsive?

Dr. O'Rhea:
No. Just sexually satisfied.

Patient: I'm secretly disgusted by my girlfriend - every time I get jiggy with her I can't help but notice the skids in her G-string. Should I 'dump' her?!

Dr. O'Rhea:
Not necessarily. This information makes excellent blackmail material – steal a pair for future 'negotiations'!

Patient: I've heard the colon can store pounds of poo – is that why I'm overweight?

Dr. O'Rhea:
That would be my medical diagnosis... you're full of sh*t

Patient: Is anal sex a bit like having a great dump?

Dr. O'Rhea:
I plead the 5th amendment!

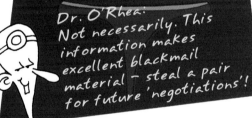
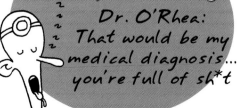

ARSEOHOLICS ANONYMOUS

Can't get through the day without a crap? Pooping in private?
Hiding nuggets around the house? Do you wake up and your first thought is about
sneaking a dump? Can't face social engagements without having a doodoo first?
Then you need to start the Arseoholics Anonymous 10 step programme:

1. We admit we are powerless over our arse - that our poops have become unmanageable.

Please help me stop farting in my dad's face.

2. Came to believe that a Pooper greater than ourselves could restore us to Sanitary.

Mine's not that hairy.

3. Made a decision to turn our lives over to the care of Bog (the toilet god).

Oh Bog. My bum is your bum.

OK. So that's two logs, six nuggets and one diarrhoea splat.

4. Made a searching and fearless bowel inventory of ourselves .

They're beige, fruity but with a smoky afterburn.

5. Admitted to Bog, to ourselves and to another human being the exact nature of our Pongs.

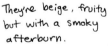

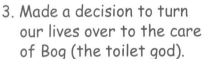
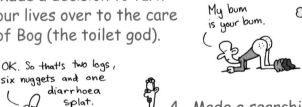

6. We're entirely ready to have Bog remove all these defects of Poo character.

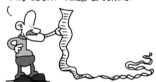

7. Make a list of all persons you have harmed, and become willing to make amends to them all.

8. Make direct amends to such people wherever possible.

9. Maintain a poo inventory and share any lapses with others.

10. When you do guff, promptly admit it.

A TOUCHING GUIDE FOR
New Poorents

Everything You Always Wanted To Know About
Human Repooduction But Were Too Ladyboy To Ask

How are poobies made? Tee hee!
Does it hurt the first time? (If you're lucky it should hurt every time)
Will there be blood? (Yes, if you try hard enough)
Should you always use protection... against splashback? (Men prefer not to)
What makes sextuplets? (Who cares - you can sell your story to a tabloid,
or give them up for adoption)

Haven't the foggiest. But we do know what happens after a prune and
a cabbage see each other across a crowded stomach and sneak off to get
jiggy in the alimentary canal...

What To Expect in Delivery

If you've been good you'll experience hours of sublime pain, followed by a
few seconds of slippery relief as you jettison your special little guy in to
your partner's arms. But middle-class hygiene-fixated trendies prefer
old-fashioned water births (down the pan). There may or may not be a
mucous cord attached to your new offspring which can be severed with
scissors or your fingers. Many couples like to make a home movie of this
wonderful event - you can make a lotta money on the internet.

Oh God, it's ugly!
Suck it back in!

AAEEEEE!!

Immediately After Delivery

Swaddle your new-born in
luxurious loo paper, though
if it is less attractive than
you were hoping for, cheap
stuff will serve it right.

She's got your eyes.

Sharing Your Delight With Family And Friends And Passers-by
(Or How To Turn Into A Total Bore)

- Talk non-stop about your newborn - mostly in arguing about who it looks most like
- Brag about how quickly it learnt to walk (though everyone knows poos can't walk - unless you tie them to a string)
- Buy it designer clothes and toys though all it wants to play with is an old loo roll tube
- Boast about its first words "Splash" and "PHFLGH"- a shameless lie since all poops have only partially-developed vocal chords and cannot speak

Once The Novelty Value Of Your New Born Has Worn Off

Some new poorents never tire of their new poopie (1%). But for the rest, the drying-out factor and loss of smell leads them to ditch the dirt and poocreate yet again.

Have a nice life, my precious.

Immediately After Delivery

Some modern women don't desire to gestate a poop for 9 hours either due to not eating enough to actually conceive a poopie, or fearing it may hamper their career (little realising that producing fine craps will raise their male boss's regard for them). For these barren bowels, there are alternatives:

- SURROGACY: paying someone else to produce a crap for you, although it's highly likely they'll selfishly want to keep the offspring.
- ADOPTION: believe it or not, there are many unwanted poopies - from mixed veg backgrounds, those that have been produced illegitimately (laxatives), or one night stands with a dodgy kebab. Most who choose adoption find it hard to bond with their adoptee.

- POO-SNATCHING: This is illoogal, but the main reason for not using this method is the chance of breaking the newborn as you snatch it from its gawping poorent.

The A to Z of Poo!

A is for arse

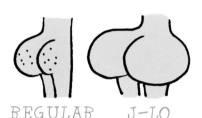

REGULAR   J-LO

B is for bottyburps

UUURP!!

Excuse me.

C is for constipation

D is for diarrhoea

E is for eye-watering

NNNGGG!

F is for floater

G is for groan

H is for hairy

I is for iceberg

J is for jaw-dropper

K is for Krakatoa

L is for log

M is for moist wipe

N is for no-show

O is for OUCH!

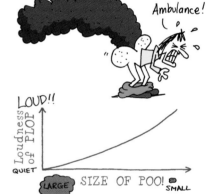

P is for plop!

Q is for quake

R is for rabbit droppings

S is for splashback

T is for talented

U is for unexpected

V is for vanishing poo

W is for wipe, wipe, wipe, wipe...

X is for xmas poo

Y is for yo-yo

Z is for zombie poo (done by old ladies)

Arsercise
IT'S TIME TO WORK THAT BUTT, BABY!

To live well into your 30s, you must look after your health, and since all doctors agree that the bottom is the most important organ, you must take extra special care of it... with a healthy diet of high fat, carbohydrates and beer and regular Arsercise – the latest fitness craze sweeping the United States of Americarse. Perform these arsercises daily and you'll see the difference in years:

THE WARM UP

WARM UP FOR 3 EARTH MINUTES WHILE YOU HYDRATE YOURSELF FULLY BEFORE WORKING OUT

GLUG
GLUG
GLUG

THE SQUAT

HOVER OVER TOILET SEAT AND HOLD POSITION FOR AS LONG AS IT TAKES.

THE SQUEEZE

REPEAT INDEFINITELY UNTIL YOU CAN BEAR HOLDING ON NO MORE, OR IMPLODE.

SQUEEZE!

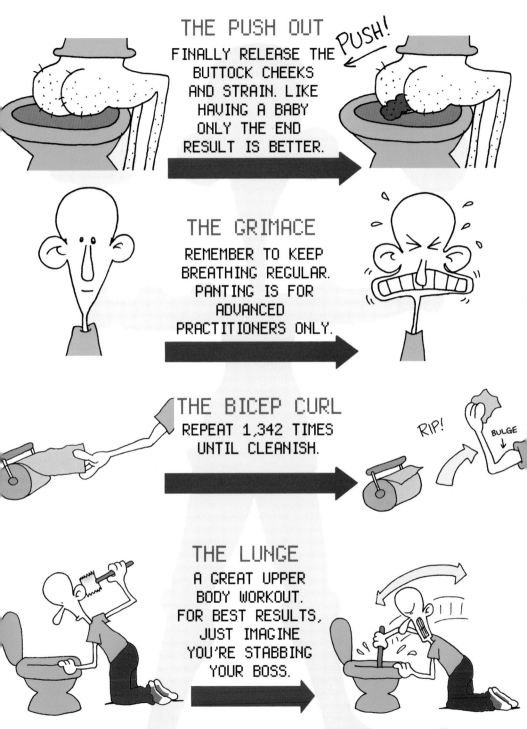

POO SPORTS

How we all woke up in history lessons when we learnt how sports like football began - some scallywag's severed head acting as the ball. Or how tennis began life as a bogey-flicking dual, or that in the 13th century rugby was Pass-the-Colostomy-Bag. So, in the future (3 years and 147 days to be precise) all our favourite sports will evolve to feature poo. You'll see.

FOOTBALL

…will be known as Phewball. The ball will be replaced with, obviously, a large Saturday-morning crap (hand-moulded if necessary) and the goalposts will be giant urinals. The red card will be awarded to the good sport who commits the biggest poo. The offside rule will mean the poo-er must have at least one sheet of paper between them and their bottie before they pull their shorts up.

PING PONG

Paddles will be replaced by bog brushes and only the sacred stinky poos of the constipated vegetarian will be used as the ball in this revamped version of table tennis. Will be renamed 'PONG PONG'. Gas masks obligatory.

TIDDLYWINKS

Tiddlywinks will be substituted by those rabbity poos you do when you're 103 years old (visit and old folk's home). Players shall attempt to aim their "Tiddlyshits", as they will now be called, into the open mouth of a sleeping relative.

SNORE!

PLINK!

TEN PIN BOWLING

...will become Ten Poo Bowling and will feature long jaggy poo pins that, due to stickiness, are almost impossible to knock down. The ball will be replaced with a loo roll that shall be thrown at the pins. Anyone who knocks a poo down will be awarded a Wedgie.

KNOCK AND RUN

...will evolve into Drop and RUNS! Contestants will perform the trots on a doorstep and scarper - not forgetting to ring the doorbell first.

Maude!
Have you been ordering crap out of the catalogue again!

TEE HEE HEE

THE LIFESTYLE
POO GURU

THIS ANCIENT CISTERN POOLOSOPHY HAS INSPIRED THE LATEST LIFESTOOL MOVEMENT, FUNG SHIT. HERE THE LEADING POO GURU OFFERS RELATIVELY FREE ADVICE* FOR THOSE WISHING TO CHANNEL THEIR OWN NATURAL ENERGY, POOP, INTO THEIR STRESSFUL LIVES TO BRING PEACE AND HARMONY!

WORSHIP:

FIRSTLY, CREATE YOUR OWN PRIVATE ALTAR, CROSS YOURSELF WITH BOWELY WATER AND OFFER GIFTS OF AIR FRESHENER AND WET WIPES TO YOUR DIVINE INSPIRATION.

SEND CHEQUES TO PO BOX 123, LONDINIUM

WATER:

SHARE YOUR TRANQUIL WATER FEATURE WITH MANKIND BY 'BLESSING' HOUSE PLANTS WHEREVER YOU GO.

PSSSSSSSS!

TINKLE!

AAH! IT'S SO RESTFUL!

AIR:

LEAVE ALL DOORS OPEN AS THIS ALLOWS THE FREE MOVEMENT OF POO SPIRIT TO PERMEATE EVERY AIR MOLECULE, FABRIC AND NOSTRIL OF YOUR HOME.

EARTH:

BECOME ONE WITH THE EARTH BY RECYCLING YOUR BOTTOM-PRODUCE AS GARDEN FERTILISER. YOUR FLOWERS WILL NEVER BE THE SAME AGAIN!

FIRE:

DON'T WASTE MONEY ON EXPENSIVE BBQ CHARCOAL- POO BRIQUETTES ARE FREE, AND FLAVOUR FOOD WITH A UNIQUE SPICY PUNGENCY.

PROSPERITY:

BELIEVE IT OR NOT THERE ARE SOME SICK FREAKS OUT THERE WHO LIKE TO WATCH PEOPLE POOING. TAKE ADVANTAGE OF THEIR PERVERSION AND SELL YOUR SERVICES TO THE SICKOS (SEE YELLOW PAGES UNDER FAECES FETISH).

LUCK:

INCREASE LUCK BY EATING A RABBIT'S FOOT (WITH A FOUR LEAF CLOVER SIDE SALAD) AND TURN THE SPECIAL POO INTO A KEY FOB. YOU'LL BE AMAZED AT THE RESULTS!

HOW TO BAKE
THE PERFECT POO!
by Delia Jeff

Ingredients:
  ½ cabbage
  a handful of sprouts
  1 tin of baked beans
  several cheap beers
  salt & pepper to taste
  a dash of laxatives
sweetcorn optional as it will mysteriously appear anyway

Utensils:
  1 large toilet bowl (if nothing else is to hand, a urinal will suffice)
  palette knife in case of sticking

Method:
Chop ingredients vaguely in mouth, mix with saliva concentrate if available, and swallow. Leave to stew in bowels for several hours at 37.4°F until aromas develop. Remove carefully from anus ring, taking care not to break it - use a palette knife if stuck and leave to cool.

Serving Suggestion:
Present as one large helping, or as individual servings.
Sprinkle with fresh quilted loo paper for a special occasion.

Seasonal Variations:
At Xmas, add turkey to the recipe for added depth and intensity.

Drinks Idea:
Wash down with half a bottle of bleach.

(serving suggestion)

Plop Psychology Quiz

What kind of shit are you? (Or save yourself the time doing this pointless quiz and ask your so-called "friends")

Question One

When you've achieved a particularly smelly poo, do you...

    a) use the air freshener before it even hits the water

    b) stay in the bog until the smell disappointingly disappears

    c) open the door, waft it, to fragrance the entire house

    d) bottle it

Question Two

If the loo roll is nearly finished, do you...

    a) waddle around the house, pants round ankles, looking for spare

    b) er, who needs loo roll?

    c) finish it, don't replace it and hide the spare...tee hee

    d) scream blue murder until emergency help arrives

Question Three

You leave a skidmark in the bowl, do you...

    a) see a Rorschach ink picture

    b) clean it 2,000m times whilst gagging 3,000 times

    c) cover it with an Everest of paper, leave it and block the system

    d) "pretend" to clean it with bog brush whilst actually making it worse

       (bonus points for returning brush dirty to holder)

Question Four

You execute a turd sooo big, it won't flush, do you...

    a) perform a Bruce Lee with the bog brush

    b) call your friends, relatives and neighbours

       round to admire it

    c) taxidermy the beauty and mount in glass case

    d) move house

Question Five

In public toilets, do you...

    a) let rip - making as much noise as possible

    b) pee/poo in mega slow motion to reduce noise disturbance

    c) dribble all over the seat, tee hee

    d) public toilets?!! You'd rather do it in your pants.

Question Six

A baby has done a woopsie, do you...

    a) check out the nappy contents like a scientist

    b) run round screaming like a girl when the nappy comes off

    c) what's the big deal, you crap your pants all the time

    d) congratulate the offending nipper on its wanton abandon

Question Seven

If you should be so lucky to get the squits on holiday, do you...

a) regret it, because it all happens too fast to properly enjoy it

b) think of the money you've saved on colonic irrigation

c) not leave your room for fear of "accidents"

d) go on as many excursions as possible - you're
    an adrenalin junkie

Question Eight

When it comes to animal poop, do you...

    a) take a picture/home movie

    b) spend hours at the zoo just in case

    c) peek in dog litter bins for a cheap thrill

    d) pray to be reincarnated as an elephant

Scores!

Q1 a=1; b=3; c=4; d=2
Q2 a=2; b=1; c=3; d=4
Q3 a=4; b=2; c=1; d=3
Q4 a=3; b=2; c=1; d=4
Q5 a=2; b=3; c=4; d=1
Q6 a=4; b=3; c=2; d=1
Q7 a=3; b=2; c=1; d=4
Q8 a=2; b=1; c=3; d=4

4-8 points   =   you're so repressed, you make Queen Victoria look like a pole dancing ladyboy gimp

9-18 points   =   hmm, could try harder

18-25 points =   full (skid)marks for effort

26-871 points =   you don't honestly think we bothered to work these points out properly, do you?

The REAL Brownies!

The Brownies may be a boring club designed by parents to get their dweeby kids off their hands for the day, but the REAL Brownies are much more fun! In fact, you're already a member! How many badges have YOU earned so far....?

TAKE THE PLEDGE

I promise that I will
Poo my best
To Love my Log
To serve the Cistern
And my U-bend
To help other Poopers
And keep the
Brownie Guide Law

LIVE THE MOTTO!

"Be Prepared" for every pooping opportunity – all you need is bags of enthusiasm, determination, friends to lean on in times of need, and a smile! Not to mention the compulsory, over-expensive uniform (there's only one reason why it's brown!).

BOBBLE HAT
Handy for storing poops when you're caught short.

YELLOW NECK TIE
Is actually a moist bum wipe. Washable.

ELASTICATED SKIRT
Only elastication will do when you <u>really</u> need to go!!

BUM BAG
Contents: One fishing net, one camera for capturing your beauties, and a mirror for getting the perfect view!

WATERPROOF BOOTS
Well, accidents will happen!

EARN YOUR BADGES!

ARTIST
Decorate your bowl with fancy shapes and colourful patterns. It's painting by numbers - number 2s!

ATHLETE
Only the fittest sphincter will be awarded this. Get in training by placing nuts between cheeks and squeezing - give the shelled nuts to grateful grandparents.

BELLRINGER
Put a bell by the loo and chime away to announce the birth of your brownie baby, or waddle seductively downstairs and ring the doorbell.

BOOK LOVER
Awarded to those who can spend many impressively unhygienic hours reading anything to hand - books, air freshener labels, towel washing instructions.

CANOEIST
You're a champion at sailing your unsinkable k(y)ack down the white water of the U-bend.

CONSERVATION
A tireless campaigner for S.O.S. (Save One's Shit), you've never pulled the flusher voluntarily.

CRIME PREVENTION
You understand it's a heinous crime to be constipated so you avoid fibre at all costs. A truly gifted individual.

DANCER
You've shown real promise in jigging whilst waiting for the loo. Michael Flatulence eat your heart out.

DISCOVERER
You've shown admirable ingenuity in the search for hidden skidmarks: from pants to sheets to your mate's stupidly white settee. A veritable Scott of the Arseantics.

FIRST AID
Your ceaseless and prompt action with medical cream/mayonnaise has saved many piles from EXCESSIVE agony.

FISHING
"It was this big, honest!" is too seldom believed, so you've demonstrated real skill in fishing your 8-incher out, stuffing and mounting it.

ANIMAL LOVER
Well done for collecting 316 samples of animal poopie and fashioning it into an attractive necklace (but you'd have scored extra if you'd thought of using the rabbit droppings as earrings).

GARDENER
Everyone will be presented with this award eventually when you've been locked out, and nature calls and you think no-one's around.

HOSTESS
Unfaltering in your efforts to host the perfect poo - velvet soft paper, soft tone light-bulb, one touch freshener, moist wipes. Bless you.

JESTER
You've shown true commitment to the humiliation of others with cling film over the seat, fake dog poo on the carpet, chocolate sauce in brother's underwear.

PHOTOGRAPHER
What Picture Messaging was invented for. You've shown real promise in snapping your stools for all to envy. Say "Faeces".

SWIMMER
Your poops have always been at home in the water, very buoyant, especially in public swimming pools, yes - you, you know who you are.

SURVIVAL
Brown Ow! You bring new meaning to "If at first you don't succeed, cry and cry again".

THE ODD SQUAD'S
FART GALLERY

1. THE SQUEAKY

HIGH-PITCHED, LONG-LASTING, NO SMELL. COMMONLY DONE BY WOMEN.

2. THE RUMBLER

SOUNDS LIKE A DISTANT RUMBLE OF THUNDER. SMELL SEEPS OUT OVER SEVERAL HOURS. COMMONLY DONE BY OLD PEOPLE.

3. THE RASPER

A SHORT SHARP BLAST BEST PERFORMED ON PLASTIC SEATS. GOOD FOR SCARING AWAY KIDS.

4. THE SQUELCHER

FAST UNDERWEAR CHANGE REQUIRED IMMEDIATELY!

A HANDY GUIDE FOR A
SERIAL FARTER!

1. TRY NOT TO BLOW OFF IN ENCLOSED SPACES!

2. STOP BLAMING THE DOG – YOU'RE NOT FOOLING ANYONE!

3.

PUT A SMALL WHISTLE BETWEEN YOUR BUM CHEEKS TO ALERT EVERYONE OF SILENT BUT VIOLENT FARTS!

4.

NEVER LIGHT YOUR FARTS IN CASE OF INTERNAL COMBUSTION!

5.

WEAR UNDERPANTS IN SHADES OF BROWN IN CASE OF FOLLOW THROUGH MISHAPS!

NEXT TIME: 'A Handy Guide for a Bum Bandit'

LIKE CRACKERS AND CHEESE, MORECOMBE AND WISE, S AND M...THE POO WOULDN'T BE THE SAME WITHOUT IT'S FRIEND THE FART. BUT THE QUESTION IS...

WHAT KIND OF FARTER ARE YOU?

FUMP!

TOOT!

EEP!

THE SNEAKY FARTER

SNEAKS UP IN STEALTH MODE AND DROPS A HOT ONE.

SSSSSS

FUMP!

THE EMBARRASSED FARTER

HOLDS IT IN UNTIL NO-ONE IN A 5-MILE RADIUS IS PRESENT.

THE 'ALL MOUTH NO TROUSERS' FARTER

GATHERS EVERYONE TO HEAR THEIR 'BIG FART' ONLY TO LET OFF A DISAPPOINTING SQUEAK.

EEP!

THE THROWER

CATCHES FARTS IN THEIR HAND AND THROWS THEM IN YOUR FACE. PURE EVIL.

THE 'NEVER FARTS' FARTER

CLAIMS TO NEVER HAVE FARTED IN THEIR ENTIRE LIFE. (USUALLY FEMALE) WILL ONE DAY EXPLODE.

THE MASTER BLASTER

LIFTS LEG AS HIGH AS POSSIBLE AND LETS RIP, KNOCKING ORNAMENTS AND CHILDREN FOR SIX.

HOW YOUR POOS CHANGE AS YOU GET OLDER!

BABY POO

LIKE NUCLEAR CABBAGE ONLY MORE DEADLY. DO NOT LET IT COME IN CONTACT WITH SKIN.

TEENAGE POO

JUST A BIG BALL OF LARD. MADE FROM A DIET OF BURGERS, PIZZAS AND CHOCOLATE. HIGHLY INFECTIOUS.

TWENTY SOMETHING POO

POO IS GREEN DUE TO SUDDEN HEALTH KICK. BUT MORE VEG IN DIET MEANS SMELLIER POOS.

THIRTYSOMETHING POO

AN INCREASE IN DINNER PARTIES MEANS POOS BECOME DARKER AND RICHER IN QUALITY. THE BOUQUET IS ALMOST PLEASANT.

FORTYSOMETHING POO

MIDDLE AGE SPREAD SETS IN. POOS BECOME HUGE, SWOLLEN MONSTROSITIES. JUST LIKE THEIR BIG ARSES.

O.A.P. (Old Aged Poo)

POOS ARE GREY, WRINKLY, DRIED UP, AND SMELL LIKE ROTTING FLESH. JUST LIKE AN OLD PERSON REALLY!

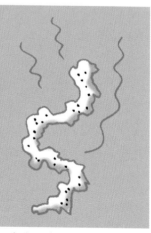

THE GREAT TAKEAWAY FOOD POO TEST!

THE CHINESE MEAL POO

NICE AT THE TIME BUT ULTIMATELY UNSATISFYING. YOU'LL FEEL LIKE ANOTHER ONE IN HALF AN HOUR.

THE MCBURGER POO

DRY, OVERCOOKED, AND EACH POO IS IDENTICAL. WARNING: MAY CONTAIN TEENAGE STAFF'S BOGIES! MMM, BOGIES...

THE FISH & CHIPS POO

A SUCCULENT POO WITH A CRISPY OUTER COATING. ACCOMPANIED BY A SIDE PORTION OF MUSHY PEE POO!

THE INDIAN MEAL POO

A REAL ARSE BURNER. SITTING DOWN WILL BE IMPOSSIBLE FOR WEEKS. KEEP FIRE EXTINGUISHER HANDY.

THE DODGY BURGER VAN POO

THE FASTEST POO IN THE WEST. FOOD GOES FROM MOUTH TO BUM IN 3.5 MINUTES DUE TO 99% GERM CONTENT. SMELLS OF WET ONIONS.

THPPPPPPPTT!!!!!

THE KEBAB POO

FOUL-SMELLING, SLIMY, GROTESQUE APPEARANCE. JUST LIKE A KEBAB, REALLY!

THE ULTIMATE GUIDE TO POO

'THE SLIPPY'

SLIPS OUT IN ONE, SWIFT MOVEMENT. REQUIRES NO WIPING.

"THE STINKER'

REEKS SO BAD YOU DON'T EVEN RECOGNISE THE SMELL.

'THE NEVERENDING STORY'

AN AMAZING ACHIEVEMENT. MAY NEED TO STAND TO ACCOMPLISH FULL LENGTH.

'THE BLIP'

SMALL BUT CAUSES BIG SPLASH.

'THE POPPETS'

COME OUT LIKE MACHINE GUN BULLETS.

'THE STEAMY HEAPY'

WILL NEVER FLUSH.

'THE FIREBALL'

HOT AND PAINFUL.
MAY SINGE
BOTTOM HAIRS.

'THE SWEETCORN'

MOST COLOURFUL
AND ATTRACTIVE.

'THE STICKY'

STICKS TO HAIRS.
REQUIRES HOURS OF
WIPING.

'THE FIREHOSE'

MAINLY WATER-BASED.
CREATES HUGE MESS.

'THE CHOP OFF'

POO IS STOPPED
HALF-WAY DUE TO
PHONE RINGING ETC.

'THE JAGGY'

CAUSED BY EATING
TOO MANY CRISPS.
MAY RESULT IN
SURGERY.

'THE VEGGIE'

LOOKS AND SMELLS
EXACTLY LIKE A
VEGGIE BURGER.

'THE CROQUETTES'

CRISPY ON THE OUTSIDE
WITH A LIGHT, PUFFY
CENTRE.

A day in the life of a POO

by Alfred J. Poo the turd x

My day begins around 8am when I begin wriggling in the intestinal tract of my human host (or 'parasite' as I like to call them). I find wriggling an effective way of generating gurgling, thus tricking my host into thinking they're starving and need breakfast. You see, I like a big fry up – all that grease oils the tubes for my 'parcel-force delivery.' And all that nosh weighs heavy on their bowel. So hoorah, there's nowhere for me to go but to my private swimming pool. After bidding "adieu" to my neighbours, L.Casei Immunitas (my, they're a friendly bunch), I put on my very fashionable sweetcorn swimsuit and do a 'bomber' off the diving board ...I think you humans call it an anus!

WEEEEEE!

I love the adrenalin rush of the freefall – I just pray my pool isn't too clean. There's nothing worse to a poop than a pool full of bleach and lemon-scented Toilet Muck™. Ugh. If I'm feeling mischievous, I'll dive straight into the U-bend, thereby depriving my host the privilege of admiring their deposit. Tee hee! But more often than not, I'll practise my "Dead Goldfish" synchronised swimming movement. Also, call me kinky but I'm quite keen on receiving the golden shower that usually accompanies splashdown. Being dirty's in my genes I guess! But ironically, the whole experience can be just like a spa treatment – being hosed down by a urinary jet, then covered in warm, muddy blankets of loo roll. I prefer recycled because then I can fantasise about where it's been!!

Then, the 'Jacuzzi' gets turned on as my proud host reluctantly pulls the flusher. Weeheeeee! Round and round I spin in an eddy of peey bubbles. If I've been

good (over-indulged and put on weight), I won't disappear the first time, which means I can indulge in a spot of S&M. Ooh-er missus! I love being beaten with the bog brush. All those bristles. Ouch. Ooh. The climax for me is to be spanked so hard, I break in two - then I'll have a companion for the day, my genetic clone!

Young poos these days! No respect!

WHOOOOOSH!

Next, it's time for the water park - those sewer chutes are wicked. Twisting and turning, what a high. And the smell? Heaven! I may meet a few old friends along the way... Grandpa Constipation Nugget clinging for dear fossilised life on the brickwork... Or that slapper, Aunty Diarrhoea spreading herself about a bit (nothing changes!).

Sometimes I'll make new pals, I still keep in touch with Nathan the Alligator who was flushed when he got too big. Nice dude. A bit needy. I'll float on my back for a while, practise my "Jaws" impersonation. I'd love to appear on "Stars in their Arse". Well, a turd can dream. But I'll come crashing back to earth when I arrive at my destination. It's paradise to me, though – the coast off Seaton Carew. Bliss. The water's beautiful... icy cold (brings a youthful flushed tone to my skin), salty (excellent for skin complaints like turd fissures) and, most importantly of all, full of pollution. What more could a jobby ask for?

The End!

NEXT WEEK:
A day in the life
of a Colostomy Bag!

Cinderella

nce upon a grime-covered toilet, Cinders (so-called because she once over-enthusiastically lit her own fart) was scrubbing away, dreaming of going to the ball. But there was fat chance of that as her bulimic step-sisters had made a right mess of the loo and it was taking forever to clean. Yet, loo and behold, the Fairly Bogmother appeared in a spray of air freshener and told Cinders she was going to the ball! Waving her magic bog brush, she transformed Cinders' rags into a Versarses number and turned the loo roll into a Lootus.

However, at the ball Cinders was so excited to be asked to dance by the inbred Prince that she pooped herself and ran off. The impressed Prince picked up the poop and scoured the land in search of its owner. Eventually he found Maude and, lo, the poo fit her bum hole perfectly! But the marriage only lasted 3 months as it turned out the prince was actually a raving woofter.

THE END!

It fits!

Little Red Riding Hood

One fine day Little Red Riding Hood was walking through the woods to visit her boring grandmother when she skidded in a turd left by an inconsiderate wolf, breaking her neck. Serves her right - hoods are soooo last spring!

THE END!

SLIP!

CRACK!

The Princess and the Poo

No wonder I couldn't sleep. Although my back feels better.

A month ago, a Princess was staying in a dodgy B&B and couldn't get to sleep - what with the smell of old smoke and sex, the polyester stained top blanket and the fear of the morning cuppa from the hospitality tray made with mini cartons of foul milk - oh, and best not forget to mention the lumpy mattress, the reason for the whole story!

So the Princess pulled back the mattress to discover a poop left by the previous occupant. Charming. In the morning, when the maids were spraying the sheets with freshener, they discovered their favourite mattress poop had been stolen. But all the mini toiletries that reeked of pine disinfectant were still there!

THE END!

Goldilocks and the 3 Bears

In a land, fart fart away, Goldilocks was in the forest looking for truffles to flog to poncey restaurants when the urge to dump over-whelmed her… Fortunately, there was a house nearby she could break into, so Goldilocks shimmied up the drainpipe and climbed in through an open window.

The first toilet she came to was a potty, so she whisked her knicks off and shouted "Timber", but the potty was way too small for her big ass so she had to waddle to the next room, where she found a urinal.   But it wasn't in the right position and Goldilocks ended up making a mess. So she waddled to the next room, where she found the perfect toilet…
three empty porridge bowls!

THE END (of the bears!)

Jeff and the Beanstalk

nce upoo a time, Jeff was zig-zagging home after a night on the bevvy & eating a dodgy beanburger, when he got those waterbed gurglings that mean only one thing. Luxurious squits. So Jeff let rip in a nearby field and then zag-zigged merrily off in the direction he'd just come. Of course, the next day, curiosity got the better of Jeff and he felt compelled to return to the scene of the slime. And do you know what? Where Jeff had fertilised the earth, there now grew a humongous weed, as tall as a skyscraper. Like all men, Jeff felt compelled to climb. Up and up he climbed. But he was still a bit hung over and lost his balance. Poor Jeff was street pizza.

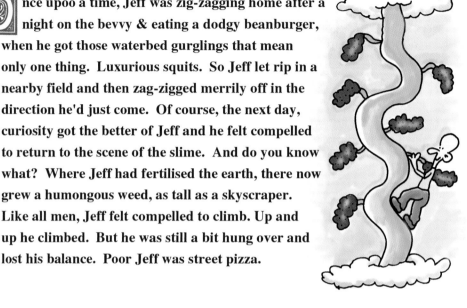

The Ugly Duckling

here once was an ugly duckling with feathers all stubby and brown... around its bottom. You see, his mother had never potty trained him properly so now none of the other ducklings wanted to play with the stinky dangleberry. Serves him right.

Farts and Crafts projects

KILL TWO TURDS WITH ONE MOAN – RECYCLE ALL THOSE OLD LOO TUBES AND CREATE FASHIONABLE ACCESSORIES TO ENHANCE YOUR LAVATORIAL EXPERIENCE. THERE IS AN ARSETIST IN ALL OF US!

DIY GAS MASK

SLIT EMPTY LOO TUBE TO CREATE TWO FLAPS. COVER OPPOSITE END WITH CLINGFILM*. PLACE FLAP OPENING OVER NOSE AND MOUTH TO CREATE AN UN-AIRTIGHT SEAL. HOLD IN PLACE WITH HAND OR SELLOTAPE (BONUS SIDE-EFFECT: SELLOTAPE GIVES A MOUSTACHE WAXING FOR THE LADIES)

CAN'T....
.... BREATHE!

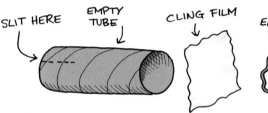

SLIT HERE — EMPTY TUBE — CLING FILM — ELASTIC BAND

*pierce to avoid suffocation. Authors accept little responsibility for maker's failure to comply with common sense.

EYE PROTECTORS

CUT TUBE IN HALF AND THREAD KNICKER ELASTIC FROM GRANNY'S KNICKERS CLUMSILY THROUGH HOLES TO FASHION GOGGLES. THEY NOT ONLY PROTECT EYES FROM POTENTIAL STINGING DUE TO EXTREME STENCH, BUT ALSO LEAVE SEXY AND TRENDY "SCARS" ON FACE.

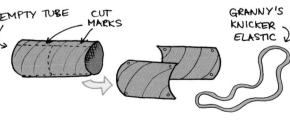

EMPTY TUBE — CUT MARKS — GRANNY'S KNICKER ELASTIC

AROMA DISTRIBUTER

TAKE OLD MAGAZINE STUFFED BESIDE TOILET
COVERED IN DUST AND GOODNESS KNOWS WHAT,
AND REMOVE PAGE. FOLD INTO A FAN
(HAPHAZARDLY TOWARDS THE END AS BOREDOM
SETS IN) AND THEN WAFT PONG
VICTORIOUSLY FOR ALL TO SAVOUR!

Is the dinner WAFT! on?

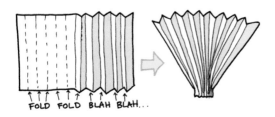

FOLD FOLD BLAH BLAH...

THE FANFARE

EITHER COLLECT DISCARDED TUBES
FOR SEVERAL WEEKS OR INSTIGATE A
BOUT OF DIARRHOEA BY VISITING GRUBBY
LOCAL KEBAB SHOP. FASHION TUBES
INTO A TRUMPET AND HERALD THE
ARRIVAL OF YOUR CHOCOLATE
STAGECOACH.

PARAP PARAH!

KSH!

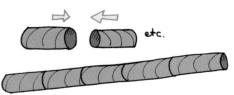

etc.

THE DUMPOLENE

WE ALL SECRETLY ENJOY THE SURPRISE OF THE SPLASHBACK – AND WHAT TURD
WOULDN'T RELISH THE THRILL OF THEIR VERY OWN TRAMPOLINE. SO, YOU SCRATCH
YOUR POO'S BACK AND IT CAN SCRATCH YOURS. JUST REMEMBER TO JUMP UP
QUICKLY TO MARVEL AT THEIR FORWARD SOMERSAULT WITH PIKE.

CLING FILM

BOING! BOING! BOING!

POO PAL

ALL TURDS, BIG AND SMALL, ENJOY A PLAYMATE IN THE WATER. TAKE TWO SWEETCORN KERNELS, GLUE TOGETHER WITH ONE FRESHLY PICKED BOGIE AND DRAW A FACE AND WINGS TO CREATE A TINY YELLOW DUCK! AFTER ALL, SWEETCORN IS A POO'S BEST FRIEND.

CHANGING FLUMES

POOR POOS. THEY SPEND JUST SECONDS ON EARTH, PLUMMETING TO THEIR WATERY GRAVE. YOU OWE IT TO YOUR TURD TO HELP THEM MAXIMISE THEIR BRIEF EXISTENCE BY MAKING THEM THIS EXHILARATING LOG FLUME

A) CUT OLD LOO TUBES IN HALF
B) STICK TOGETHER IN SPIRAL FORMATION
C) PLACE OVER ARSE AND WEE-HEE-HEE

WEEE!

TOY-LETS

GIVE YOUR POOS A STYLISH MAKEOVER. CUT OUT THESE DECORATIVE CUTTERS AND PLACE OVER YOUR SPHINCTER TO CREATE CRAZY FUN TURD SHAPES. POOING NEED NEVER BE ANAL AGAIN!

SPOOGHETTI

THE CHOCOLATE STARFISH

THE BUTT KISSER

THE POOQUET

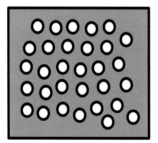

GINGERBREAD MAN

THE POODLE

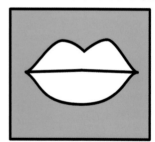

LOO ROLL ORIGAMI

Pass the minutes whilst you wait to pass the parcel with these step-by-step origami creations using simple loo paper...

"The Still Sea"

Instructions:
1. Tear off single sheet
2. Lay flat
3. Tra-la
(Difficulty rating:
  easy-poosy)

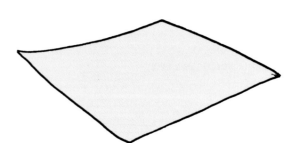

"The Yellow Squit Road"

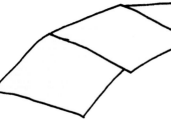

Instructions:
1. Tear off several sheets
2. Er, that's it

"The Tent"

FOLD

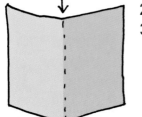

Instructions:
1. Tear off a sheet
2. Fold into triangle tent-shape
3. Find homeless mouse to live in it

Thankyou!

"The Carnation"

Instructions:
1. Remove several sheets from roll
2. Scrumple enthusiastically
3. Give to a loved one (or someone you've sinned against)

"The Intellectual"

Instructions:
1. Remove one sheet from roll of the poolosopher's inspiration
2. Adorn one's head with 'mortarboard'
3. Intellectualise away

"The Surgeon"

Instructions:
1. Make incision along dotted line and slit open
2. Place over mouth
3. Inhale until you turn blue

"Imaginary Popcorn Holder"

Instructions:
1. Take one sheet
2. Twist into cone shape
3. Glue in place with bogey (Can also be used to pretend to be a Womble)

"The Eiffel Tower"

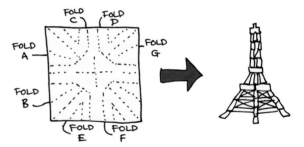

FOLD C
FOLD D
FOLD A
FOLD G
FOLD B
FOLD E
FOLD F

Instructions:
1. Fold A to B to D to C
2. Fold E to F to A to D
3. Repeat 3000 times.
4. Dur, like this is genuine.

WARNING: Thick people beware of Paper Cuts!!

The Odd Squad's
PEBBLE DASH GAME!

Ready, Steady...Squirt!

BUBBLE! SQUIRT!

You let out a massive fart next to someone smoking. The resulting blast sends you flying forward 4 spaces!

BOOM!!

You stop to help an old granny draw her pension but the smell of poo reminds her of a story which takes her 8 hours to tell. Miss a turn.

...And my poo was eight feet long and no-one believed me and....

You pause for a second to contemplate how poo is the force which unifies us all. How, no matter what our social status or intellectual rank, we all must drop our pants and squeeze out a chocolate sausage. Miss a turn.

RULES:
Last night you washed down a vindaloo with fourteen pints of lager and you have to go now! Can you run to the toilet before you ruin those new undies?!!

What you need: One dice, One marker per player (use toilet roll tubes).

How to play: First to splat their load on the loo wins!

The person you fancy is across the street. Afraid to have them see you with squidgy pants you hide in a nearby phone box but pass out from the stench of wee. Miss a turn.

POO PARTY GAMES!

BIRTHDAYS, WEDDINGS, HAMSTER FUNERALS...THROW A PARTY YOUR GUESTS WON'T BE ABLE TO FORGET - EVEN AFTER HYPNOTHERAPY!

PASS THE POO!

CEREMONIOUSLY WRAP THE SPECIAL, FRESHLY-LAID PARTY POOP IN TOILET PAPER AND VOLUNTEER TO BE THE BORE WHO DOES THE MUSIC. KEEP SCHTUM AS YOUR UNSUSPECTING GUESTS PASS ROUND THE MYSTERIOUSLY WARM PARCEL. "NO, IT ISN'T A CROISSANT" YOU TELL THEM, LAUGHING GAYLY!

Quick! Quick!

PIN THE POO ON THE I.B.S. SUFFERER

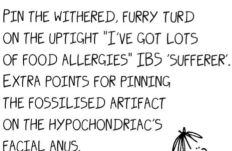

PIN THE WITHERED, FURRY TURD ON THE UPTIGHT "I'VE GOT LOTS OF FOOD ALLERGIES" IBS 'SUFFERER'. EXTRA POINTS FOR PINNING THE FOSSILISED ARTIFACT ON THE HYPOCHONDRIAC'S FACIAL ANUS.

POOSICAL STATUES!

WHEN THE TOILET WATER STOPS FLUSHING, STRIKE A GRIMACE AND FREEZE.
(MEN BE WARNED: WOMEN HAVE AN UNFAIR ADVANTAGE AS THEY ARE SKILLED
AT SQUATTING FOR HOURS IN PUBLIC INCONVENIENCES...THOUGH MEN ARE ALSO
QUITE ADEPT AT BEING IMMOBILE.)

Jeff moved!

POO DUNKING!

JOSTLE GOOD-NATUREDLY OR PUNCH YOUR WAY TO BE THE FIRST TO DUNK.
GRAB THE WHOOPSIE WITH YOUR MOUTH AND ENJOY A REFRESHING
FACIAL AT THE SAME TIME. THE WINNER GETS TB!

Got one!

BLIND MAN'S GUFF!

BE THE JILLY GOULDEN OF THE FART WORLD - SEE IF YOU CAN GUESS THE OWNER OF THE AROMA. DOUBLE POINTS IF YOU CAN GUESS WHAT THEY HAD FOR DINNER! NOTE: VICTIMS OF FOLLOW-THROUGH ARE ENTITLED TO SEEK DAMAGES. (PERSONAL INJURIES LEGISLATION CLAUSE 46, SECTION 8, PARAGRAPH 3.)

HIDE AND REEK!

A GAME FOR ONE PLAYER ONLY. HIDE YOUR TURD IN YOUR HOST'S HOUSE AND NEVER EVER TELL THEM WHY THEIR HOUSE HAS BEEN CONDEMNED BY HEALTH AND SAFETY. WHAT A WHEEZE! (NOTE: BEST HIDING PLACE IS BEHIND A RADIATOR OR A SEXY UNDERWEAR DRAWER WHICH IS RARELY VISITED.)

Cut out and
hang on
door handle!

DO
NOT
DISTURD!

(Poo in progress!)

How do your poos measure up?

TURDOMETER

Beep Beep Boooooooo...

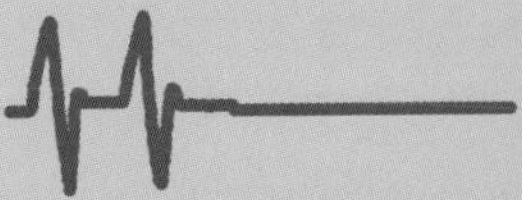

PHONE AN
AMBULANCE!

TIDAL WAVE!

GET THE
CAMERA!

NOW YOU'RE
TALKING

MUST TRY
HARDER

BAH, HUMBUG!

Poo Certificates

Cut out and give to the worthy pooer!

This is to certify that

....

is the world record
holder for

THE WORLD'S STINKIEST POO

laid on the

....

and witnessed by

....

(RECENTLY
DECEASED)

This is to certify that

....

is the world record
holder for

WORLD'S BIGGEST HUMAN DUMP EVER

dropped on

....

measuring an impressive

....

POO PUZZLES

Who knew poo could be this much fun?!!

D	I	A	R	R	H	O	E	A	P
S	E	U	P	M	U	B	S	E	C
T	N	F	L	O	A	T	E	R	O
I	E	A	E	B	O	A	S	T	W
N	S	E	I	C	T	P	O	L	P
K	R	C	J	I	A	L	S	I	A
D	A	E	H	E	L	T	R	U	T
U	X	S	H	I	T	E	I	G	W
M	A	N	U	R	E	A	P	O	O
P	I	L	E	S	J	R	W	W	N

Find these words in the grid:

TEAR   PLOP   TURTLEHEAD
MANURE   SHIT   POO   PILES
PEE   DUMP   DIARRHOEA
FLOATER   SHITE   FAECES
ARSE   BUM   BOAST
COWPAT   STINK

DOT TO DOT

Join the dots to discover what happens when you
mix twenty beers with an extra hot vindaloo!

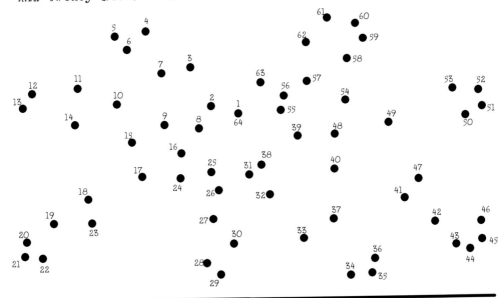

GET THE POO IN THE BOWL

Which path will take
our lonely poo to his
beloved home?

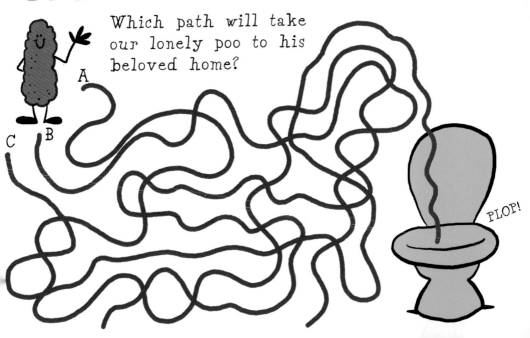

PLOP!

SPOT THE DIFFERENCE

Can you spot 12 differences between these two pictures of Jeff's proudest day?!

SPOT THE ODD ONE OUT!

  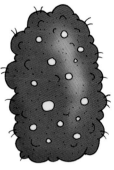 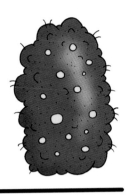

WORD SWAP

Change the piping hot pizza into a piping hot poo in only five steps!

P	I	Z	Z	A
J	O	B	B	Y

MATCH the POO to the ANIMAL!

SEXUAL HEALING

Ooh, now let's get down to shite
Baby I'm hot just like an oven
I need some pushin'
And baby, I can't hold it much longer
It's getting stronger and stronger
And when I get that feeling

I want Rectal Heaving
Rectal Heaving, oh baby
Makes me feel so fine
Helps to relieve my behind
Rectal Heaving baby, is good for me
Rectal Heaving is something
that's good for me

WANNABEE

Ow, I'll tell you what I want,
what I really really (grunt)
So tell me wheat you (grunt),
what you really really (grunt)
I'll tell you what I (grunt),
what I really really (grunt)

So tell me what you want,
what you really really want
I wannagh, I wannagh,
I wannagh, I wannagh,
I wannagh really really wanna
shit-a-shit-aghhhhh...

POO IN THE MOVIES

BEHIND EVERY GREAT FILM IS AN EVEN GREATER STORY ABOUT POO THAT THE STUDIOS THOUGHT WAS JUST TOO POWERFUL/RADICAL/TOUCHING/SEXY TO MAKE. JUST WHERE DID YOU THINK THE INSPIRATION FOR THE DESIGN OF POPCORN CAME FROM!?

THE DAMBUSTERS

1945. A BUNCH OF ENGLISHMEN WERE IN GERMANY FOR A BEER FESTIVAL AND DECIDED TO BROWN-BOMB THE TOILETS. THE LAGER-FUELLED CANNON BALLS WERE TOO STRONG FOR THE LOCAL LOOS AND BOUNCED THEIR WAY TO THE RESERVOIR WHERE THEY SMASHED THE DAM, CAUSING A HUGE FLOOD. SO THANKS TO POO WE WON THE WAR!

GONE WITH THE WIND

A FRIGID GIRL WOULDN'T BE WITH THE MAN OF HER DREAMS JUST BECAUSE HE HAD CHRONIC FLATULENCE. BUT HE DIDN'T WANT TO BE WITH HER EITHER BECAUSE HER CRINOLINE WAS ALWAYS GETTING CAUGHT IN HER SUSPICIOUSLY LESS-THAN-WHITE PANTALOONS.

(HISTORY LESSON: CRINOLINES MADE IT IMPOSSIBLE TO POO QUICKLY, THEREFORE PANTALOONS WERE INVENTED TO STORE WEEKS' WORTH OF POO)

JAWS

A MIDDLE-AGED POLICEMAN CAN'T BE BOTHERED TO GO BACK TO SHORE TO RELIEVE HIMSELF SO HE DROPS HIS LOAD IN THE SEA. HOWEVER, IT TERRORISES THE SPINELESS LOCALS AS IT BOBS MERRILY ALONG, UNINTENTIONALLY KILLING OFF SEVERAL BATHERS WITH STOMACH INFECTIONS.

CITIZEN KANE

MAN BUYS NEWSPAPER THAT HE CALLS "THE BUM" SO HE CAN PRINT PAGE AFTER PAGE OF GRATUITOUS NAKED CRAP. IT'S BRILLIANT.

THE WIZARD OF OZ

"HEALTHY EATER" (IE. SHE HAD AN EATING DISORDER) DOROTHY PASSES OUT WHILST STRAINING IN CONSPITATED AGONY. UNCONSCIOUS, SHE DREAMS OF VISITING A WIZARD WHO CAN GIVE HER A TURD. ON THE WAY SHE MEETS A LION WITHOUT A SPHINCTER AND A TIN MAN WITHOUT A FART (THE SCARECROW DIED IN A FREAK FART-LIGHTING ACCIDENT). WHEN SHE WAKES UP DOROTHY DISCOVERS SHE'S POOPED THE BED.

THE TEXAS CHAINSAW MASSACRE

A GANG OF FREE-LOADING STUDENTS ON A LONG JOURNEY ALL NEED A POO AFTER A NIGHT ON THE CIDER, SO THEY BREAK INTO A HOUSE TO USE THE TOILET WITHOUT PERMISSION... LITTLE DO THEY KNOW IT BELONGS TO AN AGORAPHOBIC AND IT'S HER TIME OF THE MONTH! IT'S A BLOODBATH!

LORD OF THE RINGS

A DOCUMENTARY ABOUT A HAIRY SHORT-ARSE WHO MUST PROTECT HIS SPECIAL RING BEFORE TWO PERVY OLD SORCERORS GET THEIR FILTHY HANDS ON IT.

THE GODFATHER

COMEDY ABOUT THE TURTLE-HEAD OF THE ITALIAN 'CORLEONE' FAMILY WHO RUN A LAUNDERING RACKET. NOT MONEY LAUNDERING, BUT ACTUAL LAUNDERING OF BED SHEETS, SOILED BY PEOPLE FORCED TO EAT CORLEONE'S DODGY LASAGNES.

CHITTY CHITTY BANG BANG

THE CHARMING STORY OF A FAMILY OFF TO THE ZOO IN THE CAR WHEN GRANNY NEEDS HER YEARLY DUMP. THEY SPEND THE DAY LOOKING FOR A VERGE BUT EVENTUALLY SHE RESORTS TO POOPING IN THE FUEL TANK - THE FUMES ARE SO GASEOUS THE CAR EXPLODES, FLYING THROUGH THE AIR. ORIGINALLY CALLED "SHITTY SHITTY BANG BANG."

THE TERMINATOR

AN OLD BIDDY WHO DOESN'T KNOW HOW TO USE THE NO-TOUCH ELECTRONIC FLUSH MECHANISM ON A HIGH-TECH TOILET AND LEAVES A FLOATER, RESULTING IN THE PEEVED-OFF LOO ATTENDANT CHASING HER.

THE SIXTH SENSE

SPOOKY TOSH ABOUT A YOUNG BOY WHO CLAIMS "I CAN SEE POO PEOPLE". APPARENTLY WHEN OUR POOS ARE FLUSHED THEY DON'T DIE, THEY HANG AROUND IN SPIRIT FORM, HAUNTING US. SO THAT'S WHAT THAT FUNNY SMELL IS.

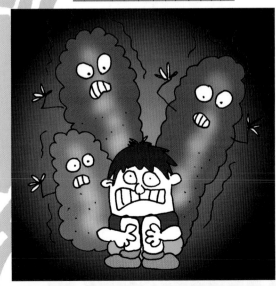

CLASSIFIED! DO NOT READ! TURN BACK NOW! OH, GO ON THEN.

CONSPOORACY THEORIES:

FIB Files 1026638004   Password: PASSWORD   Agent Name: ANUSOL

Case 1345: UFO'S   Code Name: X File

Unidentified Flying Objects my arse. Unflushable Faeces Outlaws more like. What else can you do when you're at your inlaws/friends/place of worship/whatever when you're submarine won't sink, but chuck it out the window. Extra kudos for hitting passing grannies, babies in prams or police people. Blind folk don't count - too easy a target.

Case 9927: Elvis   Code Name: BigMac

Is Elvis really still alive? Let's take a look at the fats, er facts:

a) Elvis snuffed it whilst on the throne of silage.

b) Elvis spent years gorging on suicidal fast food - it was inevitable Elvis'd call his house "Greaselands"… but a typo at the printing house resulted in an altogether quite different name.

c) an open casket that allowed lesser morsels to admire that satisfied post-pooital smile.

d) the grieving widow (although Prissy could have been grieving the fact that she'd not have anyone so fat next to her to make her look slim any more.)

So, to sum up, of course Elvis really did snuff it. Detractors who insist otherwise are just plain jealous. After all, what a way to go. No wonder Elvis is called the King of Rock and Toilet Roll.

Case 0445: MAN ON THE MOON   Code Name: Cheese

Tricky one. Did Man really land on the moon? Firstly, one must consider why there would be any point going to the moon in the first place. Because:
a) there are no scummy public toilets to enjoy.
b) zero gravity whisks your poop off before you have a chance to fondle it.
c) there is no sound in space, so what would be the point of doing wet rasping farts. "In space no-one can hear you cream."

So, we must look to the evidence. That famous shadow on the surface of the moon. That's no shadow. But the world's greatest turtlehead. Armstrong by name, arm strong by nature.

Case 0193: WAGON WHEELS   Code Name: Size is everything

So are Wagon Wheels getting smaller or are we, the child spawn of the 70's, just bigger? But at last the truth can be uncovered:

Wagon Wheels have actually got BIGGER. You see, the manufacturer realised that the bigger the wheel, the bigger the poo, the bigger the stomach, the bigger the appetite. Supply and demand, my son. We merely THINK they're smaller 'cos WE now have to pay for them, not our parents. Tightwads.

. . . .

TOP SECRET! INFORMATION MUST NOT BE PASSED ON TO UNAUTHORISED INDIVIDUALS! WE'LL JUST DENY EVERYTHING! IT'S ALL BOLLOCKS ANYWAY!

Famous Faeces

We're all fascinated by celebrities, but one part of their lives has remained hidden - until now! Finally we can reveal...the poos of the rich and famous!!

Saddam Hussein

Walt Disney

Frankenstein

Bob Marley

Mike Tyson

Evil Knievel

Jekyll & Hyde

Kate Moss

Bill Gates

Elvis

Rolling Stones

Michael Jackson

JOBBY JOB PAGES

FOR UNEMPLOYED TURDS! FOR DOO-DOOS ON THE DOLE!

Poo-l Attendant

In addition to being a people person, the ideal candidate must be able to bob in the water without floating aids for indefinite periods of time. You will be prepared to undertake long unpredictable hours, be happy working with chlorine and flexible - with positions in both children and adult pools. In return, you will enjoy many rewards: a fragranced Jacuzzi-like working environment, an appreciative audience and being chased with a net.

HEY! ONLY DIARRHOEA IN THE FAST LANE!

Pavement Skating Rink

Equal opportunities apply: this position is open to both canine and human applicants. The chosen candidate will possess excellent pooing prowess, preferably special-ising in squits on demand.

Older candidates are welcome to apply as greying poops may lack skidiness but compensate with incontinence. You will, however be discriminated against because you smell.

Salary: 14lbs of cabbage

"Chocolate" Production Line Supplier

Following the rise in obesity, we are looking to diversify our chocolate production line with healthier non-cocoa alternatives. The victorious candidate will be small and perfectly formed, understanding the importance of the bite-size philosophy. You will ideally be slow to melt and be available to work in either a sugar coating or contain a surprise filling (preferably not savoury). Being good with children and porky women an advantage.

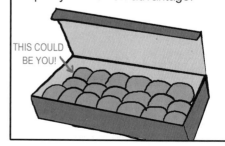

THIS COULD BE YOU!

Security to the Stars

Could you handle the limelight? Are you beefier and scarier than the average turd? Then you could be security to the stars - what could be a more effective way to repel unwanted attention than having a stinking King Kong of a turd as your bodyguard. Previous clients include Britney Poos, Cliff Retchard, and Jon Bon Jobby.

Benefits: Company sprouts and getting to sleep with groupies.

Greeting Card Carpoonist

The successful candidate can be a pretty crappy illustrator since the greeting card-buying public has very low standards. You will, however, be highly knowledgeable of all bodily functions and a skilled pun master.

But, more importantly, you will possess an hilarious wife from whom you can pinch thousands of uncredited gags. In return, you mustbe a good cook. And spray the air voluntarily after dumping.

Payment: Free envelopes

Level of drawing skill required:

Television Presenter

We all know to be a presenter you have to be full of crap, so the ultimate presenter will be 100% crap! Show those untalented wrinklies on TV the true meaning of crap presenting as you host a variety of shit shows such as 'The Weakest Stink', 'Poo Wants to be a Millionaire', and 'Ready, Steady, Cack!'

A CAMP TV SHOW HOST

A POO

The Odd Squad's
Greatest Shits

JUDGING BY ALL THE
CHOCOLATE KISSES ON THE FLOOR,
THE DOG'S BUM WAS
IN NEED OF A WASH AGAIN.

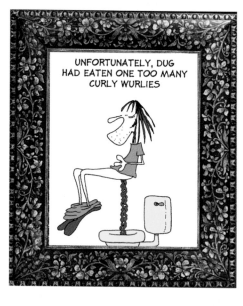

UNFORTUNATELY, DUG
HAD EATEN ONE TOO MANY
CURLY WURLIES

ONCE AGAIN,
BILLY'S GOLDFISH HAD
DIARRHOEA

BILLY COMES FIRST IN THE
SWIMMING CONTEST THANKS
TO LILY'S VINDALOO

APPARENTLY, THE DOG
HAD SWALLOWED AN
ICING BAG NOZZLE

JEFF ENTERS ANOTHER
'WIPE IT OR LEAVE IT'
DILEMMA

MAUDE DISCOVERS
SHE HAS V.P.L. (VISIBLE
POO LINE)

BILLY'S PET WORM, CYRIL,
WAS CONSTIPATED AGAIN

THE 'WHO CAN DO THE BIGGEST FART
IN THE BATH' GAME GOES AWRY
WHEN MAUDE LOSES CONTROL FOR A SECOND

JEFF FINALLY ACCEPTS
IT'S TIME TO TAKE THE DOG
OUT FOR THE TOILET

'SNOW IN JULY?
HOW STRANGE',
THOUGHT LILY

OTHER **ODD SQUAD** TITLES AVAILABLE:

TITLE	ISBN	PRICE

The Odd Squad Little Book of...series

BOOZE	1 84161 138 7	£2.50
MEN	1 84161 093 3	£2.50
OLDIES	1 84161 139 5	£2.50
POO	1 84161 096 8	£2.50
PUMPING	1 84161 140 9	£2.50
SEX	1 84161 095 X	£2.50
WOMEN	1 84161 094 1	£2.50
X-RATED CARTOONS	1 84161 141 7	£2.50
The Odd Squad Vol 1	1 85304 936 0	£3.99
The REAL Kama Sutra	1 84161 103 4	£3.99
NEW! The Odd Squad BUTT NAKED!	1 84161 190 5	£3.99

Ordering...
Please send a cheque/postal order in £ sterling, made payable to 'Ravette Publishing Ltd' for the cover price of the book/s and allow the following for postage and packing...

UK & BFPO	50p for the first book & 30p per book thereafter
Europe & Eire	£1.00 for the first book & 50p per book thereafter
Rest of the world	£1.80 for the first book & 80p per book thereafter

RAVETTE PUBLISHING LTD
Unit 3, Tristar Centre
Star Road
Partridge Green
West Sussex RH13 8RA

WARNING!

THIS BOOK IS NON-EXCHANGEABLE AND NON-REFUNDABLE AND COMES WITH NO GUARANTEE.

IF YOU DON'T LIKE IT, THINK OF IT AS 128 PAGES OF ROUGH LOO ROLL!